AN ISTANBUL
ANTHOLOGY

AN ISTANBUL ANTHOLOGY

Travel Writing through the Ages

Edited by
Kaya Genç

The American University in Cairo Press
Cairo   New York

Exclusive distribution outside Egypt and North America by I.B. Tauris & Co Ltd.,
6 Salem Road, London, W2 4BU

Dar el Kutub No. 25663/14
ISBN 978 977 416 721 8

Dar el Kutub Cataloging-in-Publication Data

Genç, Kaya
    An Istanbul Anthology: Travel Writing through the Centuries / Kaya
    Genç.—Cairo: The American University in Cairo Press, 2015.
    p.   cm.
    ISBN 978 977 416 721 8
    Istanbul (Turkey) —Description and Travel
    915.632

1 2 3 4 5   19 18 17 16 15

Designed by Fatiha Bouzidi
Printed in Egypt

Contents

The Darker Parts of the City 117

Introduction

Istanbul has long been a city in transformation. Its name changed from Byzantium to Constantinople to Istanbul. Its rulers included Byzantine Emperors, Ottoman Sultans, and republican officials. It hosted the senior patriarchate of the Greek Orthodox Church, the spiritual leader of the world's Eastern Orthodox Christians, and, from 1517 to 1924, the seat of the Islamic caliphate. So is it an Islamic city? A Byzantine one? Or a modern metropolis? "All of the above" is a good answer to give to most questions about Istanbul.

In the course of these changes the city managed to preserve its magnificent scenery, history, and culture. It became an open museum of different civilizations. Travelers from Europe and America came to Istanbul to observe this curious legacy but they went further and projected their dreams of a society free from the constraints of the western world. During two centuries of touristic activity, Istanbul became not only an object of observation, but also an inspiration of oriental fantasies for the observing subject.

This book brings together writings from some of the most interesting visitors to this multifaceted city. These writers, diplomats, and tourists observed the rituals, monuments, and the mundane life of a city whose struggle to preserve its culture in the constant and often ruthless flux of change continues to this day.

The Sea and the View

Many travelers have approached Istanbul from the sea and witnessed the beauty of the city as it appeared to them, dreamlike, in between fogs.

The Proper Seat of the Empire
of the Whole World, 1745
Giacomo Casanova

Casanova traveled to Constantinople as a military merce-
nary and was fascinated by the sight of the city.

The sight offered by that city at the distance of a league
is truly wonderful; and I believe that a more magnificent
panorama cannot be found in any part of the world. It
was that splendid view which was the cause of the fall of
the Roman, and of the rise of the Greek empire. Constantine the Great, arriving at Byzantium by sea, was so much
struck with the wonderful beauty of its position, that he
exclaimed, "Here is the proper seat of the empire of the
whole world!" and in order to secure the fulfilment of his
prediction, he left Rome for Byzantium. If he had known
the prophecy of Horace, or rather if he had believed in it,
he would not have been guilty of such folly.

The Mysterious Seal, 1843
Gérard de Nerval

This city, now as always, is the mysterious seal which unites Europe to Asia. If, outwardly, it is the most beautiful city in the world, one may criticise, as so many travellers have done, the poverty of certain quarters, and the filthiness of many others. Constantinople is like the scenery in a theatre: it must be looked at from the front without going behind the scenes. There are finical Englishmen who are content to go round Seraglio point, and down the Golden Horn and the Bosphorus in a steamer, and then say: "I have seen everything worth seeing." That is going too far. But we may perhaps regret that Stamboul, which has partly lost its former appearance, is not yet, either from the point of view of healthiness or public order, comparable to the capitals of Europe. It is doubtless very difficult to make regular streets on the hills of Stamboul and the lofty promontories of Pera and Scutari, but they could be made with a better system of construction and paving. The painted houses, the zinc domes, the tapering minarets are always charming to a poet.

Mist Over the Golden Horn, 1922
Ernest Hemingway

The Golden Horn is a waterway that separates the historic center of Istanbul from the rest of the city. The waterway owes its name to its horn shape.

In the morning when you wake and see a mist over the Golden Horn with the minarets rising out of it slim and clean towards the sun and the muezzin calling the faithful to prayer in a voice that soars and dips like an aria from a Russian opera, you have the magic of the East.

Entering the City, 1875
Edmondo de Amicis

At last came glimmering through the veil some whitish spots, then the vague outline of a great height, then the scattered and vivid glitter of window panes shining in the sun, and finally Galata and Pera in full light, a mountain of many coloured houses, one above the other; a lofty city crowned with minarets, cupolas, and cypresses; upon the summit the monumental palaces of the different embassies, and the great Tower of Galata; at the foot the vast arsenal of Tophane and a forest of ships; and as the

fog receded, the city lengthened rapidly along the Bosphorus, and quarter after quarter started forth stretching from the hill tops down to the sea, vast, thickly sown with houses, and dotted with white mosques, rows of ships, little ports, palaces rising from the water; pavilions, gardens, kiosks, groves; and dimly seen in the mist beyond, the sun-gilded summits of still other quarters; a glow of colours, an exuberance of verdure, a perspective of lovely views, a grandeur, a delight, a grace to call forth the wildest exclamations. . . .

One of my dearest delights at Constantinople was to see sun rise and set, standing upon the bridge of the Sultana Validé. At dawn, in autumn, the Golden Horn is almost always covered by a light fog, behind which the city is seen vaguely, like those gauze curtains that descend upon the stage to conceal the preparations for a scenic spectacle. Scutari is quite hidden; nothing is to be seen but the dark uncertain outline of her hills. The bridge and the shores are deserted, Constantinople sleeps; the solitude and silence render the spectacle more solemn. The sky begins to grow golden behind the hills of Scutari. Upon that luminous strip are drawn, one by one, black and clear, the tops of the cypress trees in the vast cemetery, like an army of giants ranged upon the heights; and from one cape of the Golden Horn to the other, there shines a tremulous light, fine as the first murmur of the awakening city. Then behind the cypresses of the Asiatic shore comes forth an eye of fire, and suddenly the white tops of the four minarets of Saint Sophia are tinted with deep rose. In a few minutes, from hill to hill, from mosque to mosque, down to the end of the Golden Horn, all the minarets, one after the other, turn rose colour, all the domes, one by one are silvered, the flush descends from terrace to terrace, the tremulous light spreads, the great veil melts . . .

Veiled in Her "Ash-mack," 1856
Herman Melville

Melville was an ardent traveler. He kept record of his all travels, and his travel journal features the following picturesque description of Constantinople's fogs.

The fog only lifted from about the skirts of the city, which being built on a promontory, left the crown of it hidden wrapped in vapour. Could see the base & wall of St. Sophi but not the dome. It was a coy disclosure, a kind of coquetting, leaving room for the imagination & heightening the scene. Constantinople, like her Sultanas, was thus veiled in her "ash-mack."

The First Impressions, 1903
Arthur Symons

Water, camels, sand; then broader water, boats, a little station, with a veiled woman standing in a doorway; then more water and sandy grass, a few trees; then waste-land, a long line of bullocks ploughing; then, between the railway and the water, a cluster of coloured houses, mostly of wood; then trees, more waste-land, a little bay, with hills beyond; then fields, more clusters of mean houses, ploughed land, and water; at last, the wall, with its gaps and towers; a graveyard, gardens; then, between roofs and walls, the long curve of Constantinople. A dense smell, dogs, houses; then an actual seashore, with men wading barelegged in the water, and boats coming in laden with melons; then streets of houses, with fragments of turreted walls, two birds on every turret; side streets, cutting deeply between two lines of red roofs; faces of many colors, strange clothes; then, over the roofs, but close, the water, houses, domes, minarets of the city, in a flash, veiled suddenly by the walls of the station, fastened about one.

Turkey's River Thames, 1852
Théophile Gautier

When day dawned, on the Asiatic side the Bithynian Olympus, covered with eternal snows, was rising in the rosy vapours of morning with changing tints and silvery sheen. The European shore, infinitely less picturesque, was spotted with white houses and clumps of verdure, above which rose tall brick chimneys, the obelisks of industry, the ruddy material of which, seen from a distance, is a very fair imitation of the rose granite of Egypt. If I did not fear being accused of indulging in a paradox, I would say that the whole of this part recalled to me the appearance of the Thames between the Isle of Dogs and Greenwich: the sky, very milky, very opaline, almost covered with transparent haze, still further increased the illusion. . . .

The steamer stops at the entrance to the Golden Horn. A marvellous panorama is outspread before me like an operatic stage-setting in a fair sky. The Golden Horn is a gulf of which the Old Seraglio and the landing at Top Khaneh form the two ends, and which penetrates the city, built like an amphitheatre upon its two banks, as far as the Sweet Waters of Europe and the mouth of the Barbyses, a small stream which flows into it. The name of Golden Horn comes, no doubt, from the fact that it represents to the city a true cornucopia, owing to the commodity it offers to shipping, commerce, and naval construction. On the right, beyond the sea, is a huge white building, regularly pierced with several rows of windows flanked at its angles with turrets surmounted by flagstaffs. It is a barracks, the largest but not the most characteristic of Scutari, the Turkish name of the Asiatic suburb of Constantinople, which extends, ascending towards the Black Sea, from the site of the former Chrysopolis, of which no traces remain.

The Caiq, 1915
Harrison Griswold Dwight

This skiff, called a sandal, has almost ousted the true boat of the Golden Horn, which is the legendary caique. I am sorry to say it, because I do not like to see the Turks change their own customs for European ones, but truth compels me to add that I have lolled too much in gondolas to be an unbridled admirer of the caique. A gondola is infinitely more roomy and comfortable, and it has the great advantage of not forcing you to sit nose to nose with a perspiring boatman. The caique is swifter and easier in its gait, however, and, when long enough for two or three pairs of oars, not even a gondola is more graceful. Caiques still remain at the ferries higher up the Golden Horn—and grubby enough most of them are, for they have fallen greatly in the world since bridges were built and steamers began to ply.

The Bosphorus on Christmas-day, 1815
Lady Emelia Hornby

Lady Emelia Hornby, the wife of the British financial commissioner in the Ottoman Empire, was in Constantinople in 1855, during the Crimean War. British, French, and Ottoman forces fought together against Russia, resulting in the sublime sight of warships on the Bosphorus during Christmas.

We went into Pera on Christmas-day, Lord and Lady Stratford kindly taking pity on our loneliness, and asking us to dinner. I wish you could have seen the Bosphorus as it was when we embarked in our caique from the little wooden pier of Orta-kioy, the Sultan's white marble mosque shining in the morning sun. . . .

The Bosphorus on Christmas-day was particularly beautiful to us, unused now to see outward signs of a Christian people. The almost innumerable European ships were gaily dressed with flags and pennants, which fluttered in the brilliant sunshine. You may image the effect in the Sea of Marmora, with Prince's Islands like clouds rising from the sea, and, far in dreamy distance, the Asian mountains glittering with ice and snow. It was delightful to feel the warmth of spring in your caique, and to look upon shining avalanches above the clouds themselves. . . .

Several English and French men-of-war on Christmas morning were taking in from caiques famous stocks of good things to make merry; oranges, dried fruits, grapes, and Turkish sweetmeats, whose name is Legion. We passed close alongside the 'Queen,' who always gives the Sultan such a hearty salute, that she almost sends his Majesty's gilded caiques flying in the air instead of skimming

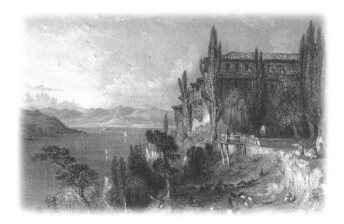

the weather. The English soldiers and sailors often give a passing countrywoman a tremendous cheer, recognising a bonnet immediately among the crowd of veila.

The Princes' Islands, 1893
Georgina Max Müller

There is a centuries-long debate about the etymology of The Princes' Islands. The Byzantine emperor Justin II built a castle and a monastery on Büyükada, the biggest of those islands, and according to one theory this was where the islands got their name. They also served as places of exile for Ottoman sultans. As more monks started living there, the islands were christened the Monk Islands. Another name used by locals was Red Islands, in reference to the color of their rocks. Although visitors failed to agree on the naming, they were united in their admiration for the beauty of the Princes' Islands.

The Princes' Islands, so called from having been a favourite resort of the Byzantine emperors, are nine in number. Four are still inhabited, the others are mere rocks, though even on some of these rocks there are the ruins of monasteries, and on each of the larger islands are several Greek monasteries, still inhabited. The Turks call these islands the 'Red Islands' from the large amount of iron which colours the rocks. We only passed close to Plate, 'the flat rock,' on which Sir H. Bulwer, when ambassador, built an Anglo-Saxon castle, of which very little remains, and where, if report is to be believed, he maintained a thoroughly Turkish establishment.

Feet in the Water, Like Venice, 1903
Arthur Symons

Stamboul, seen from the old bridge at evening, goes up like a mountain to the domes and lances of the Suleimanie. It lies with its feet in the water, like Venice; out of the water rise brown masts and spars, with furled sails, the lines fitting together into exquisite patterns; and this great, dim, coloured mass, in which certain dull reds, greys, and faint blues catch the eye, harmonises into a kind of various brown, like some rich veined wood. It is set, like Rome, on seven hills, each with its mosque, tower, or monumental ruin; at Seraglio Point it steps into the Sea of Marmora, at the mouth of the Bosporus, looking across at Asia; it stands between water and water, with the Sea of Marmora at its back, and the Golden Horn at its feet. Every conquest which has swept over it has left a ruin or a monument on its heights. Santa Sophia and the Mosque of Ahmed stand where the Hippodrome once stood; the Burnt Column, its porphyry cracked and hooped and darkened, stands, still upright, where Constantine set it; the broken aqueduct of Valens still stretches across the city of Eyoub; the Mosque of Suleiman and the Mosque of Mohammed crown the two hills where the conquerors built them; and you can follow the walls on the same track which Constantine followed when he planned the city which was to rule the East.

Trees, Plants, and Gardens

It may be hard to believe it today but Istanbul has long been famous for the beauty of its trees, plants, and lavish gardens. The construction boom of the twenty-first century threatens the city's rich natural heritage, but from private gardens to its famous Forest of Belgrade (where, incidentally, the young reformers of the empire used to meet in secret), Istanbul still offers many green sights to tourists.

Cypresses of the Little Field of the Dead, 1903
Arthur Symons

At night, as I look from my windows over Kassim Pasha, I never tire of that dull, soft colouring, green and brown, in which the brown of roofs and walls is hardly more than a shading of the green of the trees. There is the lovely curve of the hollow, with its small, square, flat houses of wood; and above, a sharp line of blue-black cypresses on the spine of the hill; then the long desert plain, with its sandy road, shutting in the horizon. Mists thicken over the valley, and wipe out its colours before the lights begin to glimmer out of it. Below, under my windows, are the cypresses of the Little Field of the Dead, vast, motionless, different every night. Last night each stood clear, tall, apart; to-night they huddle together in the mist, and seem to shudder. The sunset was brief, and the water has grown dull, like slate. Stamboul fades to a level mass of smoky purple, out of which a few minarets rise black against a grey sky with bands of orange fire. Last night, after a golden sunset, a fog of rusty iron came down, and hung poised over the jugged level of the hill.

Gardens in the Seraglio, 1716
Lady Mary Wortley Montagu

I have taken care to see as much of the Seraglio as is to be seen. It is on a point of land running into the sea; a palace of prodigious extent, but very irregular. The gardens take in a large compass of ground, full of high cypress-trees, which is all I know of them. . . .

The climate about Constantinople is delightful in the highest degree. I am now sitting, on the fourth of January, with the windows open, enjoying the warm sunshine, while you are freezing over a sad sea-coal fire; and my chamber is set out with carnations, roses, and jonquils, fresh from my garden.

The pleasure of going in a barge to Chelsea is not comparable to that of rowing upon a canal of the sea here, where, for twenty miles together, down the Bosphorus, the most beautiful variety of prospects present themselves. The Asiatic side is covered with fruit-trees, villages, and the most delightful landscapes in nature. On the European stands Constantinople, situated on seven hills. The unequal heights make it seem twice as large as it is, (though one of the largest cities in the world,) show-ing an agreeable mixture of gardens, pine and cypress trees, palaces, mosques, and public buildings . . .

Tulips in the Grand Vizier's Garden, 1726
Monsieur d'Andresel

There are 500,000 bulbs in the Grand Vizier's garden. When the Tulips are in flower and the Grand Vizier wants to show them off to the Grand Seigneur, they take care to fill in any spaces with Tulips packed from other gardens and put in bottles. At every fourth flower, candles are set into the ground at the same height as the tulips and the pathways are decorated with cages of all sorts of birds. All the trellis-work is bordered with flowers in vases and lit up by a vast number of crystal lamps of various colours. Greenery is brought in from the woods roundabout and used as a background behind the trellises. The colours and reflections of the lights in mirrors makes a marvel-lous effect. The illuminations are accompanied by noisy music and Turkish music lasts through all the nights that the tulips are in flower. All this is at the expense of the

Grand Vizier, who during the whole of tulip time, lodges and feeds the Grand Seigneur and his suite.

The Gardens of Stamboul, 1915
Harrison Griswold Dwight

I cannot claim to know very much about the gardens of Stamboul, though no one can walk there without continually noticing evidences of them—through gateways, over the tops of walls, wherever there is a patch of earth big enough for something green to take root. Any one, however, may know something about the gardens of the Bosphorus. The nature of the ground on which they are laid out, sloping sharply back from the water to an average height of four or five hundred feet and broken by valleys penetrating more gradually into the rolling tablelands of Thrace and Asia Minor, makes it possible to visit many of them without going into them. And the fact has had much to do with their character. Gardens already existed on the banks of the Bosphorus, of course, when the Turk arrived there, and he must have taken them very much as he found them. Plane-trees still grow which,

without any doubt, were planted by Byzantine gardeners;
and so, perhaps, were certain great stone-pines. . . .

Being unscientifically minded, I can say that the
magnolia might properly be classed among them, the
Magnolia grandiflora of our Southern States, since it
keeps its glossy leaves all winter long. One of the less
tenacious brotherhood, the plane-tree, is easily king of the
Bosphorus, reaching a girth and height that almost fit it
for the company of the great trees of California. It always
seems to me the most treey of trees, so regularly irregular
are the branches and so beautiful a pattern do they make

when the leaves are off. Limes, walnuts, chestnuts, horse-chestnuts, Lombardy poplars, acacias of various sorts, mulberries, the Japanese medlar, the dainty pomegranate, the classic bay, are also characteristic. The pale branches of the fig are always decorative, and when the leaves first begin to sprout they look in the sun like green tulips.

In the Belgrade Forest, 1716
Lady Mary Wortley Montagu

Named after Orthodox refugees who came from Belgrade in the sixteenth century, Belgrade Forest is located in the northwest of Istanbul. Locals jog and hike through the trails and it is also an ideal location for Sunday picnics.

The heats of Constantinople have driven me to this place, which perfectly answers the description of the Elysian fields. I am in the middle of a wood, consisting of fruit trees, watered by a vast number of fountains, famous for the excellency of their water, and divided into many shady walks, upon short grass, that seems to me artificial, but, I am assured, is the pure work of nature; and within view of the Black Sea, from whence we perpetually enjoy the refreshment of cool breezes, that make us insensible of the heat of the summer. The village is only inhabited by the richest amongst the Christians, who meet every night at a fountain forty paces from my house, to sing and dance.

A Picnic in the Forest, 1893
Georgina Max Müller

Early in July the Chargé d'affaires (the Ambassador was on leave of absence) proposed a picnic to the Bends near Baghcheh Keui, in the forest of Belgrad. The Bends are huge reservoirs in which the winter rains are stored for the supply of Constantinople. Those where we were to picnic are known as Sultan Mahmud's Bend and the Valideh Bend, and are formed by building solid walls of huge blocks of marble across the mouths of two valleys. The Bends are surrounded by trees, oak, beech, birch, elm, pine, sycamore, plane, &c., and on the careful pres-ervation of these woods the supply of water depends. . . .

'Large Valley' . . . is a favourite resort of the Turkish women of all classes. Here any fine afternoon one may see them sitting in groups of half a dozen or more, on their bright carpets spread under one of the huge plane-trees scattered all along the valley. . . .

A little way up the Large Valley stand two superb plane-trees, the trunks quite hollow; one of them is large enough to contain quite a good-sized room inside it, which is used as a cafe, whence the coffee is fetched which the Turkish ladies drink all day long, as they squat on their carpets in the Valley. These trees are supposed to date from the time of Godfrey of Bouillon.

A Bouquet of Flowers, 1875
Edmondo de Amicis

But all the beauty that has gone before is as nothing when we arrive before the Gulf of Buyukdere. Here is the supreme majesty and crowning glory of the Bosphorus. Here whoever has been weary of its loveliness and has irreverently expressed that feeling, will now uncover his head and ask pardon. We are in the middle of a vast lake surrounded with marvels, that make one wish to spin round like a dervish on the prow of the vessel in order to lose none of them. On the European shore, upon the slopes of a hill covered with greenery and dotted with innumerable villas, lies the city of Buyukdere: vast, and varied in colour like a bouquet of flowers. The town extends to the right as far as a small bay, or gulf within a gulf, along the edge of which lies the village of Kefele-Kioi, and behind this opens a wide valley, all green with fields, and white with houses, which leads to the great aqueduct of Mahmoud and the forest of Belgrade. It is the same valley in which, according to tradition, the army of the first Crusade encamped; and one of the seven gigantic plane trees for which the place is famous, is called the tree of Godfrey de Bouillon. From this to Kefele-Kioi, opens another bay, and beyond that is seen Terapia, lying at the foot of a dark green hill. When the eye turns from this towards Asia, it is with a sentiment of amazement.

Evergreens, 1856
Herman Melville

During his visit to Constantinople in 1856, Melville didn't fail to take a steamer from Bosphorus to Büyükdere. He was very impressed by the green view of the city.

Magnificent! The whole scene one pomp of art & Nature. Europe & Asia here show their best. A challenge of contrasts, where by the successively alternate sweeps of the shores both sides seem to retire from every new proffer of beauty, again in some grand prudery to advance with a bolder bid, and thereupon again & again retiring, neither willing to retreat from the contest of beauty.—Myrtle, Cyprus, Cedar—evergreens.

Imperial Life
and Its Pleasures

The capital of both the Byzantine and Ottoman empires, Istanbul has long fascinated its visitors with its endless reserves of imperial monuments and artefacts.

Entrance to Imperial Sights, 1915
Harrison Griswold Dwight

Seraglio Point is an Italian misnomer for the Turkish Serai Bournou—Palace Point. But a palace and gardens remain, not far away, and to them has been transferred the title of Top Kapou—Cannon Gate. Although this is now the oldest palace in Constantinople, the name of Eski Serai—the Old Palace—belongs to the site of that older one which the Conqueror built on the hill of the War Department. . . .

Certainly the garden of the Seraglio has its superb situation between the Golden Horn and the Marmora, its crescent panorama of cities, seas, and islands, and its mementoes of the past, to put it alone among the gardens of the world. Acropolis of ancient Byzantium, pleasance of Roman, Greek, and Ottoman emperors for sixteen hundred years, it is more haunted by asso-ciations than any other garden in Europe. One could make a library alone of the precious things its triple walls enclose: the column of Claudius Gothicus, the oldest Roman monument in the city; the church of St.

Irene, originally built by Constantine, whose mosaics look down as Justinian and Leo left them on the keys of conquered cities, the battle-flags of a hundred fields, the arms and trophies of the manial period of the Turks; the sarcophagus of Alexander, which is but one of the glories of the museum; the imperial library, where the MS. of Critobulus was discovered; the imperial treasury, with its jewels, coins, rare stuffs, gemmed furniture, the gifts and spoil of kings, in vaults too dim and crowded for their splendour to be seen; the sacred relics of the Prophet which Selim I captured with Egypt and which constitute the credentials of the sultans to the caliphate of Islam.

Description of the Sultan's Glorious Chambers, 1699
Aaron Hill

Aaron Hill traveled to Constantinople when he was fifteen. Britain's ambassador at the Sublime Porte, Lord Paget, helped the young man see some of the most privileged parts of the city.

The Roofs are Arch'd, and all set thick with Glittering Spires and Balls of Chrystal, rim'd about with Gold and Azure, whence in many Places hang great Golden Globes, adorn'd with Diamonds of surprising Lustre, all the sides are Richly Flagg'd in separate Panels with White, Black, Grey, Blue, Green, and other colour'd Marble, 'twixt every one of which runs one of Gold or Silver, reaching like the rest from top to bottom; all the floor is Veiny Marble, cover'd over with the finest and most costly Cloath of Gold, that can be purchas'd, neatly interwove with Twenty other different colours; close against the Wall, all around each Chamber lie large Cushions, of a black, green, blue, or crimson Velvet, embroidered in the richest manner, with the finest Pearls, some long, some round, and some of every form and magnitude; in short, no part of all those Chambers but possesses Ornaments, the most accomplish'd Grandeur of the stateliest Palaces of Europe cannot equalize.

The Harem in the Seraglio, 1915
Harrison Griswold Dwight

The entrance to the harem is under the pointed tower which catches the eye from afar. You go first into the court of the black eunuchs, narrow, high-walled on one side, overlooked on the other by a tiled porch and by a series of cells which never can have been high enough for the tiles that line them to be visible. A great hooded fireplace terminates the dark passage into which they open. Upstairs are roomier and lighter quarters, also tiled, for the superior dignitaries of this African colony. A few vestiges

of their power remain in the vestibule at the farther end of the court, in the shape of various instruments of torture. In a dark angle of this place, which communicates with the Court of the Pages and the Sultan's quarters, a lantern hanging behind a rail marks where the old valideh Kyossem was strangled with a curtain cord. Tiles of the same period as her mosque face one of the side walls with an elegant row of cypress trees. Beyond them opens another court. More tiles are there, and a lane of turf, where only the Sultan might ride, leads between the flagstones to a marble block. The interior of the harem is a labyrinth so complicated that I would have to visit it many more times to bring away any clear idea of its arrangement. There is very little of what we would call splendour in those endless rooms that sultan after sultan added to without order or plan. They contain, as true Turkish rooms should, almost no furniture. What furniture they do contain is late Empire, rather the worse for wear. Ugly European carpets cover a few floors. Stuffy European hangings drape a few windows. Gilded canopies cover a dais or two where a valideh soultan held her court—and almost the whole of a dark cupboard where a sultana did not disdain to sleep. There are ceilings more or less elaborately carved and gilded. There are big niches for braziers. There are doors inlaid with tortoise-shell and ivory and mother-of-pearl. There are wall fountains, some of them lovely with sculptured reliefs and painting. There are baths, also containing fountains, and screens of filigree marble, and marble tanks. There are, above all, tiles and tiles and tiles.

A Private Harem in Bebec, 1811
Lady Hester Stanhope

The interior of all Turkish houses is divided into two parts; the largest and best furnished of them is occupied by the women, and is called the harem; the other part, named the selamlik, consists seldom of more than two or three rooms, where the master of the house receives male visitors, and transacts business. Into the harem female visitors enter, but no other man than the husband, his and his wives' nearest relations, and now and then her physician. All the windows are barred and latticed, so that it is not only not possible to look in, but hardly possible for those inside to look out.

Attached to the harem of the house at Bebec there were a superb marble bath, a garden, and other comforts for the amusement of the imprisoned inmates. Provisions are taken in by means of a turn-about, such as is used in convents. All these contrivances are, in some measure, securities for the chastity of the women, but the greatest of all is included in the feeling, impressed upon them from their infancy, of the positive criminality of showing their faces to strangers.

Grand Signor's Concubines at the Seraglio, 1599
Master Thomas Dallam

An organ-builder from Lancashire, Master Thomas Dallam visited Constantinople in 1599 for business purposes. He was instructed to deliver an organ to the Sultan. This provided him with an excellent opportunity to see the city's most fascinating parts.

When I came to the grate the wall was very thick, and grated on both sides with iron very strongly, but through the gate I did see thirty of the Grand Signor's concubines that were playing with a ball in another court.

They wore upon their head nothing but a little cap of cloth of gold, which did but cover the crown of the head; no bands about their necks, nor anything but fair chains of pearl and a jewel hanging on their breast, and jewels in their ears. Their coats were like a soldier's mandilion, some of red satin and some of blue and some of other colours; they wore breeches of scamatie, a fine cloth made of cotton wool, as white as snow and as fine as lawn, for I could discern the skin of their thighs through it. These breeches came down to their mid-leg; some of them did wear fine cordoban buskins, and some had their legs naked, with a gold ring on the small of their leg; on their feet a velvet pantouffle, four or five inches high. I stood so long looking upon them that he which had showed me all this kindness began to be very angry with me. He made a wry mouth and stamped his foot to make me give over looking the which I was very loth to do, for the sight did please me wondrous well.

Of the Apartments of Women and the Lodgings of Eunuchs, 1699
Aaron Hill

And now we are arriv'd upon a Ground, where any Man, except the Sultan, is like Juvenal's Rara avis in terris, even as great a rarity as his black Swan, or any other Wonder; nothing here is seen but Beauty, strangely intermix'd with rough Deformity, each small Avenue leading to the Women, who inhabit this Division, being watch'd continually by Crowds of Blackamores, not only rob'd of all the strong and virile Marks of lusty Manhood by a smooth Castration or Decision rather, but elected from the most deform'd and evil countenanc'd of that untempting Race, as if the curs'd infatiate Jealousy of the lafeivious Sultans, cou'd not think the incapacitating them from amorous Practices with their distrusted Women, were sufficient to secure them, but they must inhumanely contrive a way to keep the Ladies Inclinations Chast, by the prevailing Virtue of a strong Antipathy.

The Gallery is terminated on the left by a large Door, which opens sideways into the Apartment of the Negro Eunuchs, or Black-Guard of the secluded Ladies; which extends it self strait forward, towards the Point of the Seraglio about two hundred Yards in length, and breadth proportionable; it consists of only one large Hall supported by large Vaults, wherein are all the Cellars, Landries, and Conveniences, requir'd for the service of the Ladies.

The Room is equally divided into spaces for the Eunuch's Lodging Places, and its high Arch'd Roof supported by an Hundred Marble Pillars, Fifty on a side; about the Middle opens a low Wooden Door, and lets you out upon a Gallery, which fronts the Gardens; here they Eat, Drink and Divert themselves, when out of Waiting, casting still an Eye of Observation on the Womens Actions.

Selamlik of Abdul Hamid, 1907
Arthur Conan Doyle

When Doyle visited Constantinople during a journey to the Mediterranean, he was delighted to learn that the empire's supreme ruler, Sultan Abdul Hamid, was a big fan of his work. Hamid had reportedly told Doyle to focus on his stories, which he preferred over his novels. During the Young Turk revolution that shook his authority, Hamid read aloud Doyle's stories in order to remain calm and not hear the protestors outside his palace.

In Constantinople we attended the weekly selamlik of Abdul Hamid, and saw him with his dyed beard and the ladies of his harem as they passed down to their devotions. It was an incredible sight to Western eyes to see the crowd of officers and officials, many of them fat and short of wind, who ran like dogs behind his carriage in the hope that they might catch the imperial eye. It was Ramadan, and the old Sultan sent me a message that he had read my books and that he would gladly have seen me had it not been the holy month. He interviewed me through his chamberlain and presented me with the Order of the Medjedie, and, what was more pleasing to me, he gave the Order of the Chekevat to my wife. As this is the Order of Compassion, and as my wife ever since she set foot in Constantinople had been endeavouring to feed the horde of starving dogs who roamed the streets, no gift could have been more appropriate.

The Cagaloglu Hamam, 1811
Lady Hester Stanhope

I go into a vast chamber filled with steam and lay down on the marble floor, they throw basins of water over me, soap me all over with a whisk like a horse's tail, then immerse me in a large bath, roll me up in cloths and lay me on a bed where I fall asleep and wake hungry and refreshed . . . the women make a parade of bathing; their patterns are set with pearls, the cloths they are wrapped in are worked with gold and coloured silks.

Public Procession of the Sultan, 1841
Hans Christian Andersen

First came a mounted military band, even the drummer and the man who played the cymbals were on horseback: the latter musician let the reins hang loose on the horse's neck, while he clashed the brazen plates in the sunlight. Now came the Sultan's guards, as soldierly a body of men as you would see in any Christian kingdom; then a number of splendid horses were led along, without riders, but all decked in gorgeous trappings, red, blue, and green, and all powdered with jewels. The horses danced along on their strong slender legs, tossing their heads and shaking their manes, while their red nostrils quivered like the leaf of the mimosa, and more than instinct seemed to flash from their bright eyes. Now came a mounted troop of young officers, all clad in the European costume, but wearing the fez cap; they were followed by civil and military officials, all clad in the same way; and now the Grand Vizier of the empire appeared, an old man, with a long beard of snowy whiteness. Bands of music had been posted at different points, and relieved each other at intervals. In general, pieces from Rossini's "William Tell" were played, but suddenly they were broken off, and the strains of the young Sultan's favourite march were heard. This march had been composed by the brother of Donizetti, who has been appointed band-master here. Now came the Sultan, preceded by a troop of Arabian horses still more gorgeously caparisoned than those who had gone before. Rubies and emeralds formed rosettes for the horses' ears; the morocco leather bridles were covered with precious stones, and saddles and saddle-cloths were wrought with pearls and jewels.

It seemed as though we were looking on the work of a spirit of Aladdin's lamp. Surrounded by a number of young men on foot, all displaying a feminine Oriental beauty, as if a number of Turkish women had ventured abroad without their veils, came riding on his splendid Arab horse the young "nineteen-year-old" Sultan Abdul Medjid. He wore a green coat buttoned across the chest, and wore no ornament, except one great jewel with which the bird of Paradise feather was fastened in his red fez cap. He looked very pale and thin, had melancholy features, and fixed his dark eyes firmly on the spectators, especially on the Franks. We took off our hats and bowed; the soldiers shouted out, "Long live the Emperor!" but he made not a gesture in acknowledgment of our salutes.

"Why does he not notice our salutes?" I inquired of a young Turk at my side. "He must have seen that we took off our hats."

"He looked at you," replied the Turk; "he looked at you very closely."

Tcheragan Serai, 1852
Théophile Gautier

Sultan Abdülaziz commissioned the construction of this palace which was designed and constructed by Nigoğayos Balyan and his sons, Sarkis and Hagop. Ottoman Sultans used the palace until a great fire destroyed it in 1910. Today a five-star hotel stands in its place.

We proceeded down the Bosphorus, keeping close to the European shore, which was blazing with light and bordered by the summer palaces of viziers and pachas, each distinguished by set pieces mounted upon iron frameworks and representing complicated monograms after the Oriental fashion, steamers, bouquets, flowerpots, verses from the Koran; and we came opposite the palace, Tcheragan Serai, which is composed of a main building with a pediment and slender columns, something like the Hall of the Chamber of Deputies in Paris, and two wings with trellised windows, making them look like two great cages. The name of the Sultan, written in letters of fire, blazed upon the façade, and through the open door we could see a large hall, where, amid the dazzling light of the candelabra, moved a number of opaque shadows, a prey to pious convulsions. It was the Padishah praying, surrounded by his court officers kneeling on carpets. A sound of nasal psalm-singing escaped from the hall along with the yellow reflections of the tapers, and spread out in the calm, blue night.

Marble Mausoleum of the Sultan Mahmoud, 1867
Mark Twain

We took off our shoes and went into the marble mausoleum of the Sultan Mahmoud, the neatest piece of architecture, inside, that I have seen lately. Mahmoud's tomb was covered with a black velvet pall, which was elaborately embroidered with silver; it stood within a fancy silver railing; at the sides and corners were silver candlesticks that would weigh more than a hundred pounds, and they supported candles as large as a man's leg; on the top of the sarcophagus was a fez, with a handsome diamond ornament upon it, which an attendant said cost a hundred thousand pounds, and lied like a Turk when he said it. Mahmoud's whole family were comfortably planted around him.

The Dolma Bagtche Palace, 1907
Will Seymour Monroe

Dolmabahçe Palace was built in nineteenth century by Gara-
bet Balyan and his son Nigoğayos Balyan. Sultan Abdülmecid

wanted a modern, European palace that would be different from the medieval, cold Topkapı Palace, the previous home of Ottoman Sultans.

The Dolma Bagtche Palace, on European side of the Bosporus north of the Golden Horn, was erected by Sultan Abdul-Mejid in 1853. It is a strange confusion and mingling of many orders of architecture Arabic, Greek, Roman, Gothic, and Renaissance. When seen from the water-side at a distance, the effect is not unpleasing; but a nearer view reveals its conglomerate nature. There are two richly decorated gates on the land side, but these are hidden by the huge walls. The interior is more sumptuous and costly than the outside. Its carved and gilded doors are of mahogany and cedar; bathrooms, the tubs cut from single blocks of Parian marble, are gorgeously frescoed; chimney pieces are made from costly malachite; there are mirrors with a hundred square feet of surface; a crystal candelabrum with two hundred and fifty candles; there are costly bronzes, Sevres porcelains, and rare paintings. Sultans Abdul-Mejid and Abdul-Aziz made Dolma

Bagtche their residence; but at the outbreak of the war with Russia Abdul-Hamid retreated to the security of the Yildiz Kiosk, and the costly palace has been unoccupied for thirty years.

City Walls, 1915
Harrison Griswold Dwight

The city walls were meant to protect Constantinople from foreign armies. They failed to do so but they continue to preserve the history of the city on them. Theodosios II built the Theodosian Walls between 408 and 413, the Ottomans preserved them, but during the nineteenth century some parts were destroyed. Still, great parts survive, giving Istanbul's roads an ancient flavor.

Constantinople has long been famous for her walls. About the rocky headland of Seraglio Point, which was the acropolis of the first settlers from Megara, still lie some blocks of the fortifications built by Pausanias after the battle of Plataea, when he drove the Persians out of

Byzantium and made it one of the strongest cities of the ancient world. This wall lasted until it was destroyed in 196 by the emperor Septimius Severus, in revenge upon the Byzantines for having taken the part of his rival Pescennius Niger. He also changed the name of the city to Antonina and made it subject to Perinthos, now a sleepy hamlet of the Marmora called Eregli. But he later refortified the town, on the advice of his son Caracalla. The Byzantium thus enlarged extended into the Golden Horn not quite so far as Yeni Jami, and into the Marmora no farther than the lighthouse of Seraglio Point. When in 328 Constantine the Great decided to turn Byzantium into New Rome, he carried the walls to the vicinity of the Oun Kapan-Azap Kapou bridge on one side, and on the other to the gate of Daoud Pasha, in the Psamatia quarter. He set the forum bearing his name, marked today by the so-called Burnt Cohimn, at the place where the city gate of Septimius Severus opened on to the Via Egnatia. His own city gate opened on to that road at the point now called Issa Kapoussou—the Gate of Jesus. . . .

An infinite variety of interest attaches to these walls—from the gates that pierce them, the towers that flank them at intervals of some sixty feet, the devices, monograms, and inscriptions of every period they contain, the associations they have had so much time to accumulate. . . .

When the younger Theodosius extended the walls he made the Golden Gate a part of them, but kept it as the state entrance to the city. Distinguished guests were met there—ambassadors, visiting princes, at least one Pope. Holy processions burned their incense under that archway. Through it passed emperors in splendour when they came to the purple, or when they returned victorious from war. No gateway in Europe can have seen so much of the pomp and glory of the world. Now the arches are blind, save for one small postern in the centre, and that was nearly choked by an earthquake in 1912. One Roman eagle still looks down from a high marble cornice upon the moat, empty of all but garden green, and upon a colony of Turkish gravestones that stand among cypresses where the Via Egnatia started away for the Adriatic.

The Fortress of the Seven Towers, 1915
Harrison Griswold Dwight

Sultan Mehmed II had this fortress built in 1458. It served as a treasury and archive space. More importantly, it was a state prison where ambassadors and rebellious Ottoman pashas were kept, and often executed.

On the other side there is a silent enclosure whose own day has come and gone since the last emperor passed through the Golden Gate. This is the fortress of the Seven Towers—three of which where built by the Turk-ish conqueror and connected by curtains with the city wall. In the towers are passages and cells as black as the subterranean maze of Blacherne, and they were used for the same purpose. Many are the stories of captivity in this high-walled place that have been told and remain to be told. One of them is briefly legible, in Latin, in a stone of the southeast tower, where it was cut by a Venetian in the seventeenth century. It used even to be the fashion to clap an ambassador into prison there when war broke out between his country and the Porte. Turkish state prisoners, of course, perished there without number. And one sultan, Osman II, when he was no more than eighteen, was barbarously put to death there in 1622. And all that blood and bitterness, which was so desperately the whole of reality for so many breathing men, is now but a pleasant quickening of romance for the visitor who follows a lantern through the darkness of the towers or who explores the battlements of the wall, grassy and anemone-grown in the spring, from which a magnificent view stretches of the sea and the city and the long line of ruined turrets marching up the hill.

Hippodrome, 1852
Théophile Gautier

Sultan Ahmet Square, the touristic heart of old Istanbul, is also known as 'Horse Square.' After all, the square served as a hippodrome in Byzantine times. Visitors are invited to imagine chariot racing and other festivities organized here, as they look upon the remnants of those ancient times.

Within the Hippodrome, as within an open-air mosque,
were collected the spoils of antiquity; a population of statues, numerous enough to fill a city, rose on the attics and
the pedestals, everywhere marbles and bronzes. The horses
of Lysippus, the statues of the Emperor Augustus and the
other emperors, of Diana, Juno, Pallas, Helen, Paris, Her-
cules, supreme in majesty, superhuman in beauty, all the
great art of Greece and Rome seemed to have sought a
final refuge there. The bronze horses of Corinth, carried
away by the Venetians, now prance over the gates of San
Marco; the images of the gods and goddesses, barbarously

melted down, have been scattered in the shape of bul-
lion. The Obelisk of Theodosius is the best preserved of
the three monuments standing in the Hippodrome. It is
a monolith of rose granite of Syene, nearly sixty feet in
height by six in breadth, gradually growing smaller up
to the point. A single perpendicular line of hieroglyphs,
sharply cut in, marks each of the four faces.

The Palace of the Crown-Wearer, 1915
Harrison Griswold Dwight

On top of the hill stands the well-preserved ruin known in
Turkish as Tekfour Serai, the Palace of the Crown-Wearer.
As to its real name, there has been the most fanciful variety of opinions. The palace is now generally supposed,
however, to have been built in the tenth century by Constantine Porphyrogenitus. It seems to have been separate
from the Palace of Blacherne, though on the analogy of
the Great Palace it may have belonged to the same group.
Architects as well as archaeologists take a particular interest in Tekfour Serai, because it is the only authentic piece
of domestic building left of Byzantine Constantinople.

Two Palaces: Beylerbey and Cheragan, 1907
Will Seymour Monroe

Beyond Dolma Bagtche, on the Asiatic side of the Bosporus, is the Palace of Beylerbey. It was erected by Abdul-Aziz in 1865. It is a white marble structure and has a marble quay, broken by steps leading to the Bosporus, on the water side. The interior is profusely decorated, and the ground floor is one great hall of columns, flagged with marble, from which leads a beautiful staircase. About the palace are beautiful gardens and graceful kiosks. Foreign sovereigns are sometimes entertained at Beylerbey.

The Palace of Cheragan is also the creation of that spendthrift Sultan Abdul-Aziz. It cost more than $30,000,000. Stone and stucco were disdained and only the costliest marbles were used. When Abdul-Hamid deposed Murad in 1876 he imprisoned him in this palace and no one but the confidential eunuchs of the sultan have been permitted to see the interior of Cheragan for thirty years . . . . Abdul-Aziz met his tragic end at Cheragan in 1876; and after he was deposed Murad remained a prisoner here until his recent death.

Cheragan Palace's Silent Rooms of Splendour, 1875
Edmondo de Amicis

Nothing of all the splendour remains in my memory except the Sultan's baths, made of whitest marble, sculptured with pendent flowers and stalactites, and decorated with fringes and delicate embroideries that one feared to touch, so fragile did they seem. The disposition of the rooms reminded me vaguely of the Alhambra. Our steps made no sound upon the rich carpets spread everywhere.

Now and then a eunuch pulled a cord, and a green curtain rose and displayed the Bosphorus, Asia, a thousand ships, a great light; and then all vanished again, as in a flash of lightning. The rooms seemed endless, and as each door appeared we hastened our steps; but a profound silence reigned in every part, and there was no vestige of any living being, nor rustle of garment save the sound made by the silken door-curtains as they fell behind. At last we were weary of that endless journey from one splendid empty room to another, seeing ourselves reflected in great mirrors, with the black faces of our guides and the group of silent servants, and were thankful to find ourselves again in the free air . . .

The Small House at Yildiz, 1868
Clara Erskine Clement

Yildiz Kiosk, the palace constantly occupied by Abdul Hamid II., is so small as to seem quite unsuitable for the home of a Sultan.

As it is three miles from Constantinople, he is always in retreat; and when he is seen on his way to the mosque, his emaciation and the expression of his large, sad eyes excite a sympathy one does not often feel for a person in so exalted a position. . . .

The small house at Yildiz, where Hamid is content to live, was formerly but a retreat for a summer afternoon. Hamid, however, does not require a large harem. Each year he receives the customary tribute of beautiful slaves, and leaves them to the care of his mother to be educated and married. The park surrounding Yildiz is very fine, and the views over the Bosphorus to the hills of Asia are extensive and lovely. Here the Commander of the

Faithful received the German emperor, taking the position of the Prophet, and demanding that the Mountain should come to him with more success than attended the efforts of Mohammed himself. He met the emperor and empress at the landing-place, and led them up the hill to the house that was set apart for them. He did not accompany his imperial guests to any spot outside of Yildiz. He supplied them with every luxurious means of making their excursions, but did not deviate from the daily routine of his life.

The Thousand and One Columns, 1867
Mark Twain

We visited the Thousand and One Columns. I do not know what it was originally intended for, but they said it was built for a reservoir. It is situated in the centre of Constantinople. You go down a flight of stone steps in the middle of a barren place, and there you are. You are forty feet under ground, and in the midst of a perfect wilderness of tall, slender, granite columns, of Byzantine architecture. Stand where you would, or change your position as often as you pleased, you were always a centre from which radiated a dozen long archways and colonnades that lost themselves in distance and the sombre twilight of the place. This old dried-up reservoir is occupied by a few ghostly silk-spinners now, and one of them showed me a cross cut high up in one of the pillars. I suppose he meant me to understand that the institution was there before the Turkish occupation, and I thought he made a remark to that effect; but he must have had an impediment in his speech, for I did not understand him.

The Sublime Porte, 1903
Arthur Symons

Sublime Porte (Turks call it Bab-ı Ali) is a high gate behind which the main state departments of the Ottoman Empire were located. Housing the Sultan's government, it was also in close proximity to the offices of Ottoman newspapers, which made Sublime Porte a composite of London's Downing and Fleet streets. Today, the gates open to the residence of Istanbul's governor.

Almost every morning I pass the Sublime Porte. It is a covered doorway of wood and stucco, with a frieze of green lettering, to which the pigeons often add a living frieze with their smooth bodies. Dust and stones are heaped about the Sublime Porte; grass grows between the stones of the court-yard, which rises inside like a mound, paved with cobbles. A fortune-telling woman squats in an angle of the pavement opposite, a negress, with her beads and charms laid out on a little carpet; the black face thrusts forward out of a veil tightened about it.

Piety and Holy Places

Istanbul was once the center of Orthodox Christianity. In 1517, less than a century after Mehmed II's army conquered the city, the Islamic caliphate moved from Cairo to Istanbul. This changed the outlook of the city but Istanbul's status as a multi-religious city, where you come across mosques, dervish lodges, and Jewish temples on every corner, remained intact.

A Typical Istanbul Mosque, 1915
Harrison Griswold Dwight

One thing that makes a mosque look more hospitable than a church is its arrangement. There are no seats or aisles to cut up the floor. Matting is spread there, over which are laid in winter the carpets of the country; and before you step on to this clean covering you put off your shoes from off your feet—unless you shuffle about in the big slippers that are kept in some mosques for foreign visitors. The general impression is that of a private interior magnified and dignified. The central object of this open space is the mihrab, a niche pointing toward Mecca. It is usually set in an apse which is raised a step above the level of the nave. In it is a prayer-rug for the imam, and on each side, in a brass or silver standard, an immense candle, which is lighted only on the seven holy nights of the year and during Ramazan. At the right of the mihrab, as you face it, stands the mimher, a sort of pulpit, at the top of a stairway and covered by a pointed canopy, which is used only for the noon prayer of Friday or on other special occasions . . . . The chandeliers are a noticeable feature of every mosque, hanging very low and containing not candles but glass cups of oil with a floating wick. I am afraid, however, that this soft light will be presently turned into electricity. From the chandeliers often hang ostrich eggs—emblems of eternity—and other homely ornaments.

Hagia Sophia, the Church of Divine Wisdom, 1716
Lady Mary Wortley Montagu

In Greek, Hagia Sophia means 'the Church of the Divine Wisdom.' Having served as the main church of Constantinople for centuries, Hagia Sophia was converted into a mosque in 1453, the year of the Ottoman conquest of the city. In 1934 it was declared a museum by the secular leaders of the republic. More recently, nationalist parties attempted to convert the building into a mosque again.

The dome of St. Sophia is said to be one hundred and thirteen feet diameter, built upon arches, sustained by vast pillars of marble, the pavement and staircase

marble. There are two rows of galleries, supported with pillars of party-coloured marble, and the whole roof Mosaic work, part of which decays very fast, and drops down. They presented me a handful of it; the composition seems to me a sort of glass, or that paste with which they make counterfeit jewels. They show here the tomb of the Emperor Constantine, for which they have a great veneration.

The Sweating Column, 1875
Edmondo de Amicis

Perhaps the most mythical component of Hagia Sophia is its sweating column. Placed at the northern corner, near the last door on the left, the column is always damp. Legend has it that the Virgin Mary's tears have made it so. Ancient inhabitants of the city believed that the column cured malaria. Emperor Justinian reportedly used it to get rid of his headaches. Today there are often long queues in front the sweating column. Visitors are instructed to put their fingers in the hole at its center. According to popular belief, this stops the palm of the hand from sweating.

Here the Turkish cavass struck in, and pointed out the pilaster upon which Sultan Mahmoud the Second, when he entered a conqueror into Saint Sophia, left the bloody impress of his right hand as if to seal his victory. Then he showed us, near the Mirab, the so-called cold window, from which a fresh air is always blowing, which inspires the greatest preachers of Islam with the most moving discourses. He pointed out, at another window, the famous resplendent stone, which is a slab of diaphanous marble, which glows like a piece of crystal when struck by the rays of the sun. On the left of the entrance on the north side is the sweating column; a column covered with bronze, through an aperture in which can be seen the marble always moist. And finally he showed a concave block of marble, brought from Bethlehem, in which, it is said, was laid, as soon as he was born, Sidi Ysaa, "the son of Mary, the apostle of God, the spirit that proceeds from Him, and merits honour in this world and the next." . . .

The chief marvel of the mosque is the great dome. Looked at from the nave below, it seems indeed, as Madame de Stael said of the dome of St. Peter's, like an abyss suspended over one's head. It is immensely high, has an enormous circumference, and its depth is only one-sixth of its diameter; which makes it appear still larger. At its base a gallery encircles it, and above the gallery there is a row of forty arched windows. In the top is written the sentence pronounced by Mahomet Second, as he sat on his horse in front of the high altar on the day of the taking of Constantinople: "Allah is the light of heaven and of earth;" and some of the letters, which are white upon a black ground, are nine yards long.

Night of Power in the Mosque of Sophia, 1907
Arthur Conan Doyle

We were admitted secretly and by very special favour into the great Mosque of Sophia during the sacred festival which is known as the Night of Power. It was a most marvellous spectacle as from the upper circle of pillared arches we looked down upon sixty thousand lighted lamps and twelve thousand worshippers, who made, as they rose and fell in their devotions, a sound like the wash of the sea. The priests in their high pulpits were screaming like seagulls, and fanaticism was in the air.

Churches of Constantinople, 1915
Harrison Griswold Dwight

The churches of Constantinople neither begin nor end with St. Sophia, however. The oldest of them is St. John the Baptist of the Studion, so called from the Roman senator Studius who about 463 founded a monastery near the Golden Gate. The monks by whom this monastery was first peopled belonged to the order known as the Sleepless Ones, because by a system of relays they kept up an unending series of offices. . . .

The church of St. Irene, long a Turkish armoury and now a military museum, also contains, in the narthex, a little mosaic which may be of Justinian's time. That of the apse belongs to the restoration of the church during the iconoclastic period. And in a chapel of the eighth-century church of the blessed Virgin, now Fetich Jami, where the figures of Christ and twelve prophets still look down from a golden dome, we have work of a much later period—probably the fourteenth century. But a far finer example of the work of that period is to be seen in Kahrieh Jami, once Our Saviour in the Fields. Kahrieh Jami, popularly known as the mosaic mosque, is in every way one of the most interesting monuments of Constantinople. Like Imrahor Jamisi it was originally the church of a monastery, and its history goes back as far. Like the Studion, also, it suffered from the quarrels of iconoclasm, it gave hospitality at a historic moment—namely during the last siege—to the miraculous icon of the Shower of the Way, and it fell into Turkish hands during the reign of Baiezid II. Kahrieh Jami means the Mosque of Woe, from the scenes that Kahrieh Jami were enacted there when the Turks stormed the walls.

The Mosque of Eyub, 1907
Will Seymour Monroe

The mosque of Eyub is the only one in Constantinople which may not be visited by Christians. Eyub Ansari, whom the mosque commemorates, was the standard-bearer and companion of the Prophet; and it is supposed that he was killed at the first siege of Constantinople in 668 by the Arabs. The mosque is a handsome white marble building with a large dome, several small domes, and two minarets. The tomb of Eyub, which is held in high veneration, is in the court on the west side of the mosque. At the time of their accession to the throne, the sultans come here to be girded with the sword of Osman. The honour of girding the successor of the Prophet with the sabre of the founder of the present dynasty falls to the chief of the whirling dervishes, who comes from Konia expressly for the purpose.

Sultan Achmet and Sultan Bayezid Mosques, 1852
Théophile Gautier

On leaving Saint Sophia I visited a few mosques. That of Sultan Achmet, situated near the Atmeidan, is one of the most remarkable. It has the peculiarity of possessing six minarets, which has given it in Turkish the name Alti Minareli Djami. I mention this because the fact gave rise

during the building to a difference between the Sultan and the scherif at Mecca. The scherif charged the Sultan with impiety and sacrilegious pride, for no temple in Islam must equal in splendour the holy Kaaba, which had the same number of minarets. The work was interrupted, and the mosque ran the risk of never being finished, when Sultan Achmet, like a clever man, hit upon an ingenious subterfuge to silence the fanatical iman: he caused a seventh minaret to be built at the Kaaba.

The high dome of the mosque of Achmet swells majestically amid several other smaller domes between its six square minarets encircled by trellised balconies wrought like bracelets. It is approached by a court surrounded by columns with black and white capitals and bronze bases, that support arcades forming a quadruple cloister or portico. In the centre of the court rises an exceedingly ornate fountain covered with bloom and complicated arabesques, scrolls, and knots, and covered with a cage of gilded trellis, no doubt in order to protect the purity of the water which is intended for ablutions. The style of the whole of the building is noble, pure, and recalls the finest time of Arab art, although the building is not earlier than the beginning of the seventeenth century. . . .

I need not now speak at any length of the mosque of Sultan Bayezid, which differs from this one only in some small architectural details that could be more readily indicated in a pencil sketch than in a written one. In the interior there are some fine pillars of jasper and African porphyry. Above its cloister hover continually swarms of pigeons as tame as those on the Piazza San Marco. A good old Turk stands under the Arcades with bags of vetches or millet. You buy some from him and scatter it in handfuls. Then from the domes, minarets, cornices, and capitals swoop down in many-coloured flocks thousands of doves, which light at your feet, rest on your shoulders, and slap your face with their wings. You find yourself all of a sudden the centre of a feathered waterspout.

Presently there is not a grain of millet left on the flags, and the birds, having satisfied their hunger, go back to their aerial perch, awaiting another piece of good fortune. These pigeons are the descendants of two wood-pigeons which

Sultan Bayezid once purchased of a poor woman who begged for alms, and which he presented to the mosque.

As usual with the founders of mosques, Bayezid has his turbeh near by. There he sleeps, covered with a gold and silver carpet; under his head, with a humility worthy of a Christian, a brick made of the dust collected from his clothes and hoes; for in the Koran, there is a line which runs: "He who has become covered with dust while travelling in the paths of Allah need not fear the fires of hell."

Sultan Solyman and Sultana Valida Mosques, 1716
Lady Mary Wortley Montagu

Perhaps I am in the wrong, but some Turkish mosques please me better [than St. Sophia]. That of Sultan Solyman is an exact square, with four fine towers in the angles; in the midst a noble cupola, supported with beautiful marble pillars; two lesser at the ends, supported in the same manner; the pavement and gallery round the mosque of marble; under the great cupola is a fountain, adorned with such fine coloured pillars I can hardly think them natural marble; on one side is the pulpit, of white marble, and on the other, the little gallery for the Grand Signor. A fine staircase leads to it, and it is built up with gilded lattices. At the upper end is a sort of altar, where the name of God is written; and before it stand two candlesticks, as high as a man, with wax candles as thick as three flambeaux. The pavement is spread with fine carpets, and the mosque illuminated with a vast number of lamps. The court leading to it is very spacious, with galleries of marble, of green columns, covered with twenty-eight leaded cupolas on two sides, and a fine fountain of basins in the midst of it. . . .

This description may serve for all the mosques in Constantinople. The model is exactly the same, and they only differ in largeness and richness of materials. That of the sultana Valida is the largest of all, built entirely of marble, the most prodigious, and, I think, the most beautiful structure I ever saw, be it spoken to the honour of our sex, for it was founded by the mother of Mahomet IV. Between friends, Paul's church would make a pitiful figure near it, as any of our squares would do near the atlerdan, or place of horses, (*at* signifying a horse in Turkish).

The Mosque of the Conqueror, 1907
Will Seymour Monroe

The mosque of the Conqueror crowns the fourth hill of the ancient city, and occupies the site of the historic church of the Holy Angels. Here were buried the rulers of the Byzantine empire in sarcophagi of porphyry, granite, serpentine, and marble; but their tombs were desecrated by the Latin vandals, the crusaders, who pillaged Constantinople in 1204. They converted the holy vessels into troughs for their horses; the mitres and vestments of the bishops, they made into helmets and halters; and the body of Justinian, which had reposed in the vault of the church for seven hundred years, they desecrated and robbed of its jewels.

A Masterpiece of Tile Decoration: Rustem Pasha Mosque, 1915
Harrison Griswold Dwight

[Mimar Sinan's] masterpiece in this decoration is the mosque of Rustem Pasha, son-in-law and Grand Vizier to Siiliman the Magnificent. This mosque, lifted on retaining walls above the noise of its busy quarter, has a portico which must have been magnificently tiled—judging from the panel at the left of the main door—and the whole interior is tiled to the spring of the dome. The mosque is small enough for the effect of the tiles to tell—and to be almost ruined by the fearful modern frescoes of the vaulting. The guides of Pera have a favourite legend to the effect that Rustem Pasha brought back these tiles from his wars in Persia and built a mosque for them to save giving them up to his imperial master. But no one need be an expert to see the impossibility of any such story. The tiles must have been designed for the walls which they incrust, and by a supreme master of decoration. I should not be surprised to learn that Sinan himself drew them all. There is a tall narrow panel on either side of the mosque, between two windows, which seems to me one of the most perfect ways imaginable of filling such a space. So are the spandrels of the arches supporting the gallery, and the niche of the mihrah, and the back of the mimher. All through the mosque, however, the way in which the artist has varied his designs and colours, while never losing his unity of effect, is a piece of genius.

Dervish Lodge at Pera, 1843
Gérard de Nerval

Istanbul's most famous dervish lodge still stands at the tail end of Istiklal Street in Beyoğlu. It is a monastery (Turks call it a dergah) where the sama ceremony is performed by Mevlevis. The modern republic banned all religious sects and their rituals and the lodge was turned into a museum. Today sama ceremonies are organized in the lodge for touristic purposes and they are open to everyone.

At the Pera all the dervishes wear white robes pleated like the Greek fustandles. In public performances their business is to spin round on their own axes as long as possible. All of them are clothed in white, except the chief, who wears blue. Every Tuesday and Friday the session begins with a sermon, after which all the dervishes bow before their superior, then take up positions in the hall in such a way that they can turn round without touching one another. The white skirts whirl, the head, with its felt cap, spins round, and each monk seems to be flying. Some of them play sad airs upon a reed flute. To the whirlers, as to the howlers, there comes a certain magnetic moment of exaltation which seems to produce a peculiar State of ecstasy. . . .

Even if the dervishes are pantheists, as the genuine Osmanlis suggest, this does not prevent them from having an incontestable religious title. They were established, they say, by Orchan, the second Sultan of the Turks. Seven masters founded their order, the figure being an entirely Pythagorean one which shows whence their ideas come. The general name is mewelevis from that of their original founder; that of dervishes, or durvesch simply means poor.

Whirling Dervishes, 1716
Lady Mary Wortley Montagu

Among the images of those days come the Dervishes; and the most famous of the thirty-two orders, the mevlevi, have a notable tekke in the street of Pera. I went prepared to see the luminous visages of saints, rapt in visions of Paradise. But I was under a great delusion. The famous divine fury of the dance seemed to me only a theatrical representation. They are certainly very curious to behold, as they enter the circular mosque, one behind the other, wrapped in large brown cloaks, their heads bent down, their arms concealed, accompanied by barbaric music, monotonous and sweet, resembling the sound of the wind in the cypresses of the cemeteries. And when they whirl round, and bow themselves two by two before the Mirab, their movement is so languid and majestic that you have a sudden doubt as to their sex.

A Funeral in Istanbul, 1912
Grace Mary Ellison

We Westerners, with our curious ideas of Eastern life, cannot imagine the picturesque, simple, and natural attitude the Turks have towards death. None of the hideous wailing, the rending of garments, sackcloth and ashes (supposed to be part of the Eastern mourning); none of our Western terrifying preparation for the long last journey; no mourning, no flowers, no funeral cards; it is as if the dear one had gone on a journey to a foreign land,

and his family and friends pray for him as if he were still alive. A Turkish burial, however, is impressive in its simplicity. A plain wooden coffin, covered with a Persian shawl, and a fez at its head, is carried on the shoulders of the relatives and friends.

When the dead man's eyes are closed the Hodja is called, and he reads for the comfort of the bereaved ones some verses of the Koran. Then he pauses, and solemnly asks those persons present whether they consider their relative an upright, honourable man—a curious custom, this seems to me; it is almost as if the Hodja were preparing for the dead man a passport for the next world. (I write these words with all reverence.) It is not always, however, that the assembled mourners answer the Hodja's question in the affirmative. If their conscience tells them to speak the truth they do so, and the Hodja answers simply, "Then forgive your brother his sins, as Allah will forgive you," and the assembled mourners pass on to the grave.

To me it has seemed a little strange to see the sons of wealthy Pashas buried as only the poor in our country would be buried. When I questioned a friend about this she answered, "The money you people in the West spend on funeral pomp we give to the poor assembled round the grave, and according to the deceased's years and fortune. Supposing a rich man of 83 is buried, eighty-three sovereigns would be distributed amongst the poor; when a man of 83 and of moderate means, eighty-three francs, or even eighty-three pence, as the case may be. The poor are never forgotten in this country; they come to the marriage feast, they come to the Bairam festivities, every day they come to this house and are fed, and even during death they are not neglected."

Streets, Festivities, and Commerce

Istanbul's bazaars are abuzz with tourists on the lookout for the most beautiful rugs and diamonds the city has to offer and there is no better way to experience the city's culture than on its streets, as travelers have been finding out for centuries.

Sidewalks and Streets, 1922
Ernest Hemingway

The sidewalks are so narrow that everyone has to walk in the street and the streets are like rivers. There are no traffic rules and motor cars, street cars, horse cabs and porters with enormous loads on their backs all jam up together. There are two main streets and the others are alleys. The main streets are not much better than alleys.

A Fierce and Active Struggle, 1903
Arthur Symons

To walk, in Constantinople, is like a fierce and active struggle. One should look at once before, behind, and underneath one's feet; before, behind, and underneath one's feet some danger or disgust is always threatening. I never walked up the steep road which leads from the bridge to Pera without the feeling that I was fighting my way through a hostile city. A horn blows furiously, and a black man runs up the hill, clearing the way before the dashing and struggling horses of the tram. At the same moment a cab drives at full speed down the hill, and the horses set their feet on the pavement. In front of you a man balances slices of offal on a long pole across his shoulder; they dangle before and behind; he swings cheerfully with his burden through the crowd.

Perfect Labyrinth, 1856
Herman Melville

Started alone for Constantinople and after a terrible long walk, found myself back where I started. Just like getting lost in a wood. No plans to streets. Pocket-compass. Perfect labyrinth. Narrow. Close, shut in. If one could get up aloft, it would be easy to see one's way out. If you could get up into tree. Soar out of the maze. But no. No names to the streets no more than to natural allies among the groves. No numbers. No anything.

Two Bridges, 1903
Arthur Symons

Cross either of the bridges, and you must look not less carefully to your feet. The old bridge hangs by a thread; it was broken in two, and has never been mended, only patched; in the middle, where it is some inches narrower, an iron-plated barge supports it. It sways, creaks, catches your feet, seems at every moment about to fall abroad into the water, which you see through the holes in its planks. The railing is held together by iron wire; the ends of the beams hang out ragged and broken over the water. The Grand Pont is more solidly based, but it is made of rough planks set together in irregular lengths and at uneven levels, nailed roughly, the nails standing up out of the planks. It is always in course of making; planks lie about in the road, waiting for use; men are working above great gaps, through which you see the water. As wheels rattle over it, the planks leap up under your feet; you can scarcely set foot on a plank that is not quivering. On each side is a narrow sidewalk, slightly raised, and clamped at the edge with iron. A cross-current drives at you as you walk along it; people are crowding up and down from the steamboats of the Bosporus and the Golden Horn, which have their quays moored to the right and left of the bridge. Wheels are upon you from every side; there is no rule of the road; every one fights his own way through for himself.

Istanbul Beggars, 1867
Mark Twain

A beggar in Naples who can show a foot which has all run into one horrible toe, with one shapeless nail on it, has a fortune—but such an exhibition as that would not provoke any notice in Constantinople. The man would starve. Who would pay any attention to attractions like his among the rare monsters that throng the bridges of the Golden Horn and display their deformities in the gutters of Stamboul? O, wretched impostor! How could

he stand against the three-legged woman, and the man with his eye in his cheek? How would he blush in presence of the man with fingers on his elbow? Where would he hide himself when the dwarf with seven fingers on each hand,

no upper lip, and his under-jaw gone, came down in his majesty? Bismillah! The cripples of Europe are a delusion and a fraud. The truly gifted flourish only in the by-ways of Pera and Stamboul.

The Bazaar, 1907
Will Seymour Monroe

The bazaar is the chief emporium of retail trade in a Turkish city; it is a sort of an Oriental department store. The word bazaar means "to bargain," and the institution has been appropriately named, for I found it infinitely easier to bargain than to buy at the great bazaars of Constantinople and Smyrna. The Grand Bazaar and the Egyptian Bazaar are the two best known in Constantinople. The former is really a city within a city, with arcaded streets, interminable lanes, alleys, and fountains; and all enclosed by high walls and covered by a vaulted roof that is studded with a hundred cupolas.

The business of the bazaar is classified, and a given commodity or guild has one or more streets for the display and traffic of its wares. The Grand Bazaar has

something like three thousand separate shops, and it covers a space more than a mile in circuit . . . . The shopkeepers sit cross-legged upon a bit of matting and carelessly smoke their pipes or play with their beads. There is no fixed price for anything, and every purchase involves a prolonged linguistic contest. Shopkeepers do not seem at all anxious to sell, and one may spend the whole day at the bazaar sipping coffee, eating sweetmeats, and conversing in a dozen languages. The bazaar, in fact, combines the features of a museum, theatre, and promenade, and its mercantile function seems quite secondary.

An Oriental Shop, 1852
Théophile Gautier

An Oriental shop is very different from a European one. It is a sort of alcove cut out of the wall, and closed at night with shutters that are let down like the ports of a ship. The dealer, sitting cross-legged upon a bit of matting or Smyrna carpet, idly smokes his chibouque, or counts with careless fingers the beads of his chaplet, with an impassible, indifferent look, preserving the same attitude for hours at a time, and apparently caring very little whether he has a customer or not. . . .

One thing that strikes the stranger in Constantinople is the absence of women from the shops. Mussulman jealousy does not allow of the relations which commerce involves, so it has carefully kept from business a sex in which it trusts very little. Many of the smaller household duties which are with us relegated to women are carried out in Turkey by athletic fellows with mighty biceps, curly beards, and great bull necks, a practice that, rightly enough, appears ridiculous to us.

The Balik-Bazaar and the Grand Bazaar, 1875
Edmondo de Amicis

We start from the mosque of the Sultana Validé. Here perhaps some epicurean reader would wish to stop and give a glance at the Balik-Bazaar, the fish-market, famous in the time of that Andronicus Paleologus, who, as has been recorded, drew from the fisheries along the walls of the city alone, enough to meet the culinary expenses of his entire court. Fish, indeed, is still most abundant at Constantinople, and the Balik-Bazaar in its best days, might offer to the author of the Ventre de Paris, a

subject for a pompous and appetising description, like the great suppers of the old Dutch pictures. The vendors are almost all Turks, and stand ranged around the square, with their fish piled up on mats spread on the ground, or upon long tables, around which a crowd of buyers and an army of dogs, vociferate and yelp. . . .

The Great Bazaar has nothing exteriorly to attract the eye, or give an idea of its contents. It is an immense stone edifice, of Byzantine architecture, and irregular form, surrounded by high grey walls, and surmounted by hundreds of little cupolas, covered with lead, and perforated with holes to give light to the interior. The principal entrance is an arched doorway without architectural character; no noise from without penetrates it; at four paces from the door you can still believe that within those fortress walls there is nothing but silence and solitude. But once inside you stand bewildered. It is not an edifice, but a labyrinth of arcaded streets flanked by sculptured columns and pilasters; a real city, with its mosques, fountains, crossways and squares, dimly lighted like a thick wood into which no ray of sunlight penetrates; and filled by a dense

throng of people. Every street is a bazaar, almost all leading out of one main street, with an arched roof of black
and white stone, and decorated with arabesques like the
nave of a mosque.

Smells of the Great Bazaar, 1867
Mark Twain

When you wish to buy a pair of shoes you have the swing
of the whole street—you do not have to walk yourself
down hunting stores in different localities. It is the same
with silks, antiquities, shawls, etc. The place is crowded
with people all the time, and as the gay-coloured eastern fabrics are lavishly displayed before every shop, the
Great Bazaar of Stambul is one of the sights worth seeing. It is full of life and stir and business, dirt, beggars,
asses, yelling peddlers, porters, dervishes, high-born
Turkish female shoppers, Greeks, and weird-looking and
weirdly dressed Mohammedans from the mountains and
the far provinces and the only solitary thing one does
not smell, when he is in the Great Bazaar, is something
which smells good.

The Real Rug Market, 1915
Harrison Griswold Dwight

The real rug market of Constantinople is not in the Bazaars nor yet in the bans of Mahmoud Pasha, but in the Stamboul custom-house. There the bales that come down from Persia and the Caucasus, as well as from Asia Minor and even from India and China, are opened and stored in great piles of colour, and there the wholesale dealers of Europe and America do most of their buying. The rugs are sold by the square metre in the bale, so that you may buy a hundred pieces in order to get one or two you particularly want. Burly Turkish porters or black-capped Persians are there to turn over the rugs for you, shaking out the dust of Asia into the European air. Bargaining is no less long and fierce than in the smaller affairs of the Bazaars, though both sides know better what they are up to. Perhaps it is for this reason that the sale is often made by a third party. The referee, having first obtained the consent of the principals to abide by his decision—"Have you content?" is what he asks them—makes each sign his name in a note-book, in which he then writes the compromise price, saying, "Sh-sh!" if they protest. Or else he takes a hand of each between both of his own and names the price as he shakes the hands up and down, the others crying out: "Aman! Do not scorch me!" Then coffees are served all around and everybody departs happy.

Missir Charshi and the Dried Fruit Bazaar, 1915
Harrison Griswold Dwight

There are two other covered markets, both in the vicinity of the Bridge, which I recommend to all hunters after local colour. The more important, from an architectural point of view, is called Missir Charshi, Corn or Egyptian Market, though Europeans know it as the Spice Bazaar. It consists of two vaulted stone streets that cross each other at right angles. It was so badly damaged in the earthquake of 1894 that many of its original tenants moved away, giving place to stuffy quilt and upholstery men. Enough of the former are left, however, to make a museum of strange powders and electuaries, and to fill the air with the aroma of the East. And the quaint woodwork of the shops, the dusty little ships and mosques that hang as signs above them, the decorative black frescoing of the walls, are quite as good in their way as the Bezesten. The Dried Fruit Bazaar, I am afraid, is a less permanent piece of old Stamboul. It is sure to burn up or to be torn down one of these days, because it is a section of the long street—almost the only level one in the city—that skirts the Golden Horn. I hope it will not disappear, however, before some etcher has caught the duskiness of its branching curve, with squares of sky irregularly spaced among the wooden rafters, and corresponding squares of light on the cobblestones below, and a dark side corridor or two running down to a bright perspective of water and ships.

The Slave Market, 1867
Mark Twain

Circassian and Georgian girls are still sold in Constantinople by their parents, but not publicly. The great slave marts we have all read so much about—where tender young girls were stripped for inspection, and criticised and discussed just as if they were horses at an agricultural fair—no longer exist. The exhibition and the sales are private now. Stocks are up, just at present, partly because of a brisk demand created by the recent return of the Sultan's suite from the courts of Europe; partly on account of an unusual abundance of bread-stuffs, which leaves holders untortured by hunger and enables them to hold back for high prices; and partly because buyers are too weak to bear the market, while sellers are amply prepared to bull it.

Ramadan in Istanbul

Ramadan, the ninth month of the Islamic calendar, which is observed by the city's Muslim community as a month of fasting, has long fascinated Istanbul's travelers. The bairam holiday, Eid al-Fitr, marks the end of the month, when Istanbullus celebrate their sacrifices with various festivities.

Scenes from Ramazan in Istanbul, 1852
Théophile Gautier

Ramazan, as every one knows, is half Lent, half carnival; the day is given up to austerity, the night to pleasure; penance is accompanied by debauch as a legitimate compensation. From sunrise to sunset, the exact time being marked by a cannon-shot, it is forbidden by the Koran to take any food, however light. Even smoking is forbidden, and that is the most painful of privations for a people whose lips are scarcely ever taken away from the amber mouthpiece. To quench the most burning thirst with a drop of water would be a sin, and would rob fasting of its own merit. But from evening to morning everything's permissible, and the privations of the day are amply compensated for; the Turkish city then gives itself up to fasting. . . .

During Ramazan the most complete freedom is enjoyed. The carrying of lanterns is not obligatory as at other seasons. The streets, brilliantly lighted, render this precaution needless. Giaours may remain in Constantinople until the last lights have been extinguished, a piece of boldness rather dangerous at any other time. . . .

A masked ball cannot offer a greater variety of costumes than Top Khaneh Square on a night in Ramazan. Bulgarians, in their coarse smocks and fur-trimmed caps; slender-waisted Circassians, their broad chests covered with cartridges which make them resemble organ fronts; Georgians, in short tunics belted with metal girdles, and Russian caps of varnished leather; Arnauts, wearing sleeveless embroidered jackets over their bare torsos; Jews, known by their gowns split down the side and their black caps bound with a black handkerchief; the Island Greeks, with their full trousers, their tightly drawn sashes, and their fez with silk tassel; the Reformed Turks, in frock coats and red fez; the Old Turks, wearing huge turbans, and rose-coloured, jonquil, cinnamon or sky-blue caftans, recalling the fashions of the days of the Janissaries;

Persians, in tall black astrakhan-lamb caps; Syrians, easily known by their gold striped kerchief and their white
mach'las, cut like Byzantine dalmatics; Turkish women,
draped in white yashmaks and light-coloured ferradjehs;
Armenians, less carefully veiled, wearing violet and black
shoes,—form, in groups which constantly draw together
and fall apart, the most amazing carnival imaginable.

Preparations for the Evening Meal, 1915
Harrison Griswold Dwight

Nothing is more characteristic of late afternoons in
Ramazan than the preparations for the evening meal
which preoccupy all Moslems, particularly those who
work with their hands. As the sun nears the horizon,
fires are lighted, tables are spread, bread is broken, water
is poured out, cigarettes are rolled, and hands are lifted
half-way to the mouth, in expectation of the signal that
gives liberty to eat. This breaking of the daytime fast
is called iftar, which means feast or rejoicing, and is
an institution in itself. The true iftar begins with hors-
d'oeuvres of various sorts—olives, cheese, and preserves,

with sweet simits which are rings of hard pastry, and round flaps of hot unleavened bread, called pideh. Then should come a vegetable soup, and eggs cooked with cheese or pastirma—the sausage of the country—and I know not how many other dainties peculiar to the season, served in bewildering variety and washed down, it may be, with water from the sacred well Zemzem in Mecca. Any Turkish dinner is colossal, but iftar in a great house is well nigh fatal to a foreigner. Foreigners have the better opportunity to become acquainted with them because Ramazan is the proverbial time for dinner-parties. The rich keep open house throughout the month, while the poorest make it a point to entertain their

particular friends at iftar. The last meal of the night also
has a name of its own, sohour, which is derived from the
word for dawn. Watchmen patrol the streets with drums
to wake people up in time for it, while another cannon
announces when the fast begins again.

Bairam in Istanbul, 1843
Gérard de Nerval

The following morning was the first day of Bairam.
Guns from all the forts and ships roared forth at day-
break, drowning the call of the Muezzins who hail Allah
from the tops of a thousand minarets . . . . The next
day, which was the first day of Bairam, perhaps a mil-
lion of the inhabitants of Stamboul, Scutari, Pera and
the surrounding country filled the immense triangle
which has its apex at Seraglio point . . . . Many Pera
Europeans mingled with the crowd, for in the days of
Bairam all religions have a share in the rejoicings of
the Mussulmans. It is at least a civic festival, even for
those who cannot take part wholeheartedly in the ceremonies of Islam. The Sultan's band, under the direction

of Donizetti's brother, played some very fine marches, but in unison, according to Oriental custom. The chief sight in the procession was the passing of the icoglans, or bodyguard, who wore helmets adorned with crests and great blue plumes. They looked like a forest on the march, like that of which we read in Macbeth. . . .

The square was crowded with games, sports and amusements of all kinds. After the sacrifice, everybody rushed to the food and refreshment stalls. Pastries, sweetened creams, fried dishes and kebabs—a dish beloved by the people, which is made of grilled mutton, eaten with parsley and slices of unleavened bread—were distributed to all and sundry at the cost of the principal citizens. Furthermore, anyone might go into any house and enjoy the meals which were being served there. Rich or poor, all the Mussulmans who have houses of their own, treat, as well as they can, those who come to them, without concerning themselves either about their position in life or their religion. It was, indeed, a custom followed by the Jews at the feast of the Passover.

Karagueuz, 1876
Pierre Loti

During his stay in Istanbul the French writer Pierre Loti was charmed by the experience of watching Karagueuz ('black-eye') and Hacivat ('İvaz the Pilgrim'). Characters from a shadow play performed during Ramadan Bairam, the month of festivities, Karagueuz and Hacivat have played a Punch and Judy role in the history of the Ottoman Empire.

The adventures and misdemeanours of His Lordship Karagueuz have entertained countless generations of Turks, and there is nothing to indicate that the popularity of this individual is nearing its end.

Karagueuz shares many of the traits of the old French character Polichinelle; having given everyone, including his wife, a good hiding, he in turn receives a beating from Satan, who finally carts him off, much to the delight of the spectators.

Karagueuz is made of cardboard or wood; he appears in the form of a puppet or a moving silhouette; he's equally funny as either. He adopts voices and postures Punch has never dreamed of; the caresses he lavishes upon Madame Karagueuz are irresistibly comic. Sometimes he will bawl out to the spectators and set himself at odds with them. Sometimes he's facetious (albeit in quite an ill-chosen way), and in plain view of every one he does things that would scandalise even a monkey. In Turkey it's all quite acceptable and in order, and each evening one can see decent family folk, lantern in hand, taking troupes of young children to see Karagueuz.

So it is, then, that roomfuls of infants get to watch a show that would prompt blushes in an English guard-house. It's just one of those oddities in oriental behaviour: it would be completely erroneous to be even tempted to infer that Moslems are far more depraved than we are.

Karagueuz theatres open on the first day of the lunar month of Ramazan and for thirty days they are all the rage. At the end of the month everything is dismantled and put away. For a whole year Karagueuz stays in his box and is not let out, not on any pretext whatsoever.

Kocheks and Mettaghs, 1915
Harrison Griswold Dwight

Dancing is not uncommon in the coffee-houses of the people during Ramazan. Sometimes it is performed by the gipsy girls, dressed in vivid cotton prints and jingling with sequins, who alone of their sex are immodest enough to enter a coffee-house. Dancing boys are oftener the performers—gipsies, Greeks, or Turks—who perpetuate a custom older than the satyr dances of India or the Phrygian dances of Cybele. Alimeh, whence the French ahnee, and kochek are the technical names of these not too respectable entertainers. Sometimes the habitués of the coffee-house indulge in the dancing themselves, if they are not pure Turks, forming a ring and keeping time to the sound of pipe and drum. Of recent years, however, all this sort of thing has grown rare. What has become rarer still is a form of amusement provided by the itinerant story-teller, the mettagh, who still carries on in the East the tradition of the troubadours. The stories he tells are more or less on the order of the Arabian Nights, and not very suitable for mixed companies—which for the rest are never found in coffee-shops. These men are often wonderfully clever at character monologue or dialogue. They collect their pay at a crucial moment of the action, refusing to continue until the audience has testified to the sincerity of its interest by some substantial token.

Caffeine and Nicotine

Despite modern smoking bans and the recent increase in the number of global coffee shop chains, Istanbul continues to boast of its coffee culture and nargile places, where locals happily smoke their hookahs and sip cups of Turkish coffee, served with a glass of cold water.

A Turkish Café, 1852

Théophile Gautier

The Turkish café on the Boulevard du Temple has given Parisians a false idea of the luxury of the Oriental cafés. Constantinople is very far from indulging in such wealth of horse-shoe arches, slender columns, mirrors, and ostrich-eggs. Nothing can be plainer than a Turkish café in Turkey. I shall describe one considered to be one of the finest, yet in no way recalling the luxuries of Oriental fairyland.

Imagine a room about twelve feet square, vaulted and whitewashed, surrounded with a breast-high wainscotting and a divan covered with straw matting. In the centre is the most elegantly Eastern detail, a fountain of white marble with three basins superimposed one above another, which throws into the air a jet of water that falls splashing down. In one corner blazes a brazier on which coffee is made, cup by cup, in little coffeepots of brass, just as consumers call for it.

Served in the French Manner, 1843
Gérard de Nerval

This particular café is a meeting-place for those of high Society. It might almost be a café chantant from our own Champs-Elysées. At rows of tables on either side of the road sit the fashionable and smart ladies of Pera. Everything is served in the French manner—ices, lemonade and mocha. The only piece of local colour is afforded by the presence of three or four storks which, as soon as you have asked for coffee, come and take post in front of your table like so many marks of interrogation. However, they would never venture to make an attack upon the sugar bowl with the beaks which, at the end of those long necks, seem to tower above the table. They wait respectfully. So these tame birds go from table to table collecting sugar or biscuits.

A Change in Manners, 1915
Harrison Griswold Dwight

How is it that these who burst once out of the East with so much noise and terror, who battered their way through the walls of this city and carried the green standard of the

Prophet to the gates of Vienna, sit here now rolling cigarettes and sipping little cups of coffee? Some conclude that their course is run, while others upbraid them for wasting so their time. For my part, I like to think that such extremes may argue a complexity of character for whose unfolding it would be wise to wait. I also like to think that there may be some people in the world for whom time is more than money. At any rate, it pleases me that all the people in the world are not the same. It pleases me that some are content to sit in coffee-houses, to enjoy simple pleasures, to watch common spectacles, to find that in life which every one may possess—light, growing things, the movement of water, and an outlook on the ways of men.

Women Smokers, 1852
Théophile Gautier

The smoke of latakieh and tombeki ascends in perfumed spirals from the chibouques, the narghilehs and cigarettes, for everybody, even women, smokes in Constantinople. Lighted pipes fill the darkness with brilliant dots and look like swarms of fireflies. The summons "A light!" is heard in every possible idiom, and the waiters hurry in answer to these polyglot calls, brandishing a red-hot coal at the end of a small pair of pincers.

A Greater Kick than Absinthe, 1922
Ernest Hemingway

Turks sit in front of the little coffee houses in the narrow blind-alley streets at all hours, puffing on their bubble-bubble pipes and drinking deusico, the tremendously poisonous, stomach rotting drink that has a greater kick than absinthe and is so strong that it is never consumed except with an hors d'oeuvre of some sort.

Tombeki, 1875
Edmondo de Amicis

The tobacco is displayed in pyramids, or round masses, each one surmounted by a lemon. There is the lattakia of Antioch, the Seraglio tobacco, bland and fine as the finest silk, tobacco for cigarettes and for the chibouk, of all grades of strength and flavour, from that smoked by the gigantic Galata porter, to that in use by the idle odalisque of the Imperial kiosk. The tombeki, a very strong tobacco that would go to the head of the oldest and most seasoned smoker, if its fumes did not reach the lips purified by the water of the narghile, is kept in closed glass jars, like a medicine. The tobacconists are almost all Greeks or Armenians, of ceremonious manners, affecting lordly airs; the customers stand in groups and chat; here you may see personages from the different ministries, or get an occasional nod from some great man; politics, the last bit of news, the last bit of scandal are discussed; it is a small, private and aristocratic bazaar, which invites to repose, and even in passing, gives forth a breath of the pleasure of talk and smoke.

Clubs of the Poorer Classes, 1915
Harrison Griswold Dwight

At night it is a deserted city. But just before and just after dark the coffee-houses are full of a colour which an outsider is often content to watch through lighted windows. They are the clubs of the poorer classes. Men of a street, a trade, or a province meet regularly at coffee-houses kept often by one of their own people. So much are the humbler coffee-houses frequented by a fixed clientele that the most vagrant impressionist can realise how truly the old Turkish writers called them Schools of Knowledge. Schools of knowledge they must be, indeed, for those capable of taking part in their councils. Even for one who is not, they are full of information about the people who live in Stamboul, the variety of clothes they wear, the number of dialects they speak, the infinity of places they come from.

The Exciter of Imagination, 1875

Edmondo de Amicis

Of how many imperial edicts, of how many theological-cal disputes and sanguinary struggles has not this black liquid been the cause; 'this enemy of sleep, and of fecundity'—as the more austere ulemas call it;—'this genius of dreams and exciter of the imagination,' as it is named by the ulemas of broader opinions; now, after love and tobacco, it is the dearest comfort to all, even the poorest Osmanle. Coffee is drank on the tops of the Towers of Galata and the Seraskierat, in all the steamboats, in the cemeteries, in the barbers' shops, at the baths, in the bazaars. No matter in what corner of Constantinople you may find yourself, you have only to cry out, without turning your head:—café ge! (coffee seller!) and in three minutes a cup is smoking before you.

The Darker Parts of the City

In Istanbul, life continues deep into the morning and it is the neighborhood of Pera, more than any other, that offers the most exciting opportunities of entertainment for the city's foreign dwellers.

Pera's Madmen, 1811
Lady Hester Stanhope

Those Turks, who are not very rigid in the observance of the laws of Mahomet, and who wish to drink wine or spirits, do it I believe secretly, or go to the French coffee-houses at Pera, where their intemperance is not observed: but I entirely differ from many travellers, who tell us that the major part of the Turks drink fermented liquors. I aver that no people in the world adhere more rigidly to the injunctions of their religion in that and other respects. Those who take forbidden drinks are generally soldiers, Tartars and persons of the lowest class. The effects of spirituous liquors on the Turks are remarkable. Naturally sedate, composed, and amicable, they become, when intoxicated, downright madmen; and the inhabitants of Pera, who are accustomed to see them in this state, know well the danger of getting in their way at such a moment, that they avoid them as they would a mad bull.

The Business and Shipping Centre
for the Europeans, 1907
Will Seymour Monroe

The foreign ambassadors and consuls have their quarters here; the gorgeous palaces of successful Greek, Armenian, and Hebrew financiers are also here; and most of the hotels for Europeans and Americans are in Pera. The streets are as narrow and badly paved as in Stambul; but the slopes of the hills and the wealth and position of the inhabitants tend to give the place a hygienic aspect not discerned in other parts of Constantinople. Galata is at the base of the hill on which Pera is located and it fronts on both the Golden Horn and the Bosporus. It is the business and shipping centre for the Europeans. F. Marion Crawford has well characterised Galata as the fermenting vat of the scum of the earth.

First Moments in Pera, 1876
Pierre Loti

Taxim, a busy quarter on the heights of Pera: European carriages and clothes jostling with the carriages and

costumes of the Orient: blazing heat and blazing sun: a mild breeze throws the dust and the yellowed leaves of August up in the air: the scent of the myrtles: the din of the fruit sellers: streets cluttered with grapes and water-melons . . . . The very first moments of my sojourn in Constantinople etch these images in my memory.

Being a total stranger, I would spend my afternoons beside the Taxim road, sitting in the breeze, under the trees. As I let myself drift back over the period that had just ended, my eyes absently followed the cosmopolitan stream in front of me.

Tower of Babel, 1716
Lady Mary Wortley Montagu

I live in a place, that very well represents the tower of Babel: in Pera they speak Turkish, Greek, Hebrew, Armenian, Arabic, Persian, Russian, Sclavonian, Walachian, German, Dutch, French, English, Italian, Hungarian; and, what is worse, there are ten of these languages spoken in my own family. My grooms are Arabs; my footmen French, English, and Germans; my nurse an Armenian; my house-maids Russians; half a dozen other servants, Greeks; my steward an Italian; my janizaries Turks; so that I live in the perpetual hearing of this medley of sounds, which produces a very extraordinary effect upon the people that are born here; for they learn all these languages at the same time, and without knowing any of them well enough to write or read in it. There are very few men, women, or even children here, that have not the same compass of words in five or six of them.

Galata Tower, 1852
Théophile Gautier

The Tower of Galata, in the Frankish business quarter, rises from the centre of the houses, topped by a pointed cap of verdigrised copper, and overlooks the old Genoese walls falling in ruins at its feet. Pera, the residence of the Europeans, outspreads on the top of a hill its cypresses and its stone houses, that contrast with the Turkish wooden shanties, and stretch as far as the Great Field of the Dead. . . .

I retraced my way and ascended to the Little Field of the Dead to reach Pera again. I turned off to the right, which brought me, by following the old Genoese walls,—at the foot of which is a dry moat half filled with filth in which dogs sleep and children play,—to the Galata Tower, a high building which is seen from afar off at sea, and which, like the Seraskierat Tower, has at its top a sentry watching for fires. It is a genuine Gothic donjon, crowned with battlements and topped by a pointed roof of copper oxidised by time, which, instead of a crescent, might well bear the swallow-tailed vane of a feudal manor. At the foot of the tower is a mass of low houses or huts which give an idea of its very great height.

Mussulman But Like My Own Homeland, 1843
Gérard de Nerval

From the foot of the tower of Galata with Constantinople before me, its Bosphorus and its seas again I turn my gaze towards Egypt, now long vanished from my sight. Beyond the peaceful horizon which surrounds me, over this land of Europe, Mussulman indeed, but already like my own homeland, I still feel the glory of that distant mirage which flames and raises clouds of dust in my memory, like the image of the sun which, when one has gazed upon it fixedly, pursues the tired eye, though it has plunged into the shade again. My surroundings add force to this impression: a Turkish cemetery, beneath the walls of Galata the Genoese. Behind me is an Armenian barber's shop, which is also a cafe; and huge red and yellow dogs, lying on the grass in the sun, covered with wounds and scars from their nightly battles. On my left a genuine santon, wearing his felt hat, sleeping that sleep of the blest which is for him a foreshadowing of paradise. Down below is Tophana, with its mosque, its fountain and its batteries of guns commanding the entrance to the harbour. From time to time I hear the psalms of the Greek liturgy chanted by nasal voices, and over the road which goes to Pera I see long funeral processions led by popes who wear upon their brows crowns of imperial shape. With their long beards, their robes of spangled silk, and their ornaments of imitation jewels, they look like phantoms of the sovereigns of the Later Empire.

Istanbul After Hours, 1922

Ernest Hemingway

No one who makes any pretence of conforming to custom dines in Constantinople before nine o'clock at night. The theatres open at ten. The night clubs open at two, the more respectable night clubs, that is. The disreputable night clubs open at four in the morning. . . .

All night hot sausage, fried potato and roast chestnut stands run their charcoal braziers on the sidewalk to cater to the long lines of cab men who stay up all night to solicit fares from the revellers.

Before the sun rises in the morning you can walk through the black, smooth-worn streets of Constan and rats will scuttle out of your way, a few stray dogs nose at the garbage in the gutters, and a bar of light comes through the crack in a shutter letting out a streak of light and the sound of drunken laughing. That drunken laughing is the contrast to the muezzin's beautiful, minor, soaring, swaying call to prayer, and the black, slippery, smelly offal-strewn streets of Constantinople in the early morning are the reality of the Magic of the East.

Istanbul Dogs, 1867

Mark Twain

The dogs sleep in the streets, all over the city. From one end of the street to the other, I suppose they will average about eight or ten to a block. Sometimes, of course, there are fifteen or twenty to a block. They do not belong to any body, and they seem to have no close personal friendships among each other. But they district the city themselves, and the dogs of each district, whether it be half a block in extent, or ten blocks, have to remain within its bounds. Woe to a dog if he crosses the line! His neighbours would snatch the balance of his hair off in a second. So it is said. But they don't look it.

They sleep in the streets these days. They are my compass—my guide. When I see the dogs sleep placidly on, while men, sheep, geese, and all moving things turn out and go around them, I know I am not in the great street where the hotel is, and must go further. In the Grand Rue the dogs have a sort of air of being on the lookout—an air born of being obliged to get out of the way of many carriages every day—and that expression one recognises in a moment. It does not exist upon the face of any dog without the confines of that street. All others sleep placidly and keep no watch. They would not move, though the Sultan himself passed by.

The Masters of the City, 1903
Arthur Symons

And the dogs, who are, in a sense, the masters here, have lost the sense of human relationship. Kindness restores it to them; surprise quickens their gratitude. For the most part they are left alone, and they have made laws for themselves, and taken up their own quarters. They live hardly better than the beggars; they are diseased from birth, and they lie in the streets, as the beggars lie in the streets, with all their sores, sometimes pitied a little, foul, pitiable things. With night they waken into some hideous uneasiness; and their howling, as it comes up through a silence only broken by the tapping of the bekje's iron staff, is like a sound of loud wind or water far off, waxing and waning, continually going on, and at times, as it comes across the water from Stamboul, like a sound of strings scraped and plucked savagely by an orchestra of stringed instruments.

A Fire, 1876
Pierre Loti

I walked slowly up to the house. The doors had been pushed in and the windows broken; smoke was coming out through the roof; looters had been busy, one of those ghastly mobs that crop up in Constantinople whenever there's the chance of a fight. I stepped into my home and was greeted by a rain of dirty water and soot, flakes of charred plaster and floor boarding that was still alight . . .

However, the fire had been extinguished. One room burnt out, one floor, two doors, and a partition. Aided by a big dose of sang-froid I had got the situation under control. The 'bachibozouks' had forced the pillagers to surrender their booty, then they'd cleared the square and dispersed the crowd.

Two armed 'zap ties' stood guard at my forced-in door. I entrusted to them the care of my belongings and took the ferry across to Galata.

Kief, 1875
Edmondo de Amicis

The nature, the philosophy, the entire existence of this people is signified by a particular condition of the mind and body which is called kief, and which is their supremest happiness. To have eaten sparely, to have drunk a cup of pure water, to have prayed, to feel the flesh in repose and the conscience tranquil, and to be somewhere whence can be seen a vast horizon, under the shade of a tree, following with the eye the flight of doves from a neighbouring cemetery, distant sails of vessels, the

hum of insects, the clouds of heaven, and the smoke of the narghile, vaguely ruminating upon God, on death, on the vanity of earthly things, and the sweetness of eternal rest; this is kief. To be a quiet spectator on the great world's theatre; this the Turk's highest aspiration.

A Turkish Bath, 1867
Mark Twain

I went into one of the racks and undressed. An unclean starveling wrapped a gaudy table-cloth about his loins, and hung a white rag over my shoulders. If I had had a tub then, it would have come natural to me to take in washing. I was then conducted down stairs into the wet, slippery court, and the first things that attracted my attention were my heels. My fall excited no comment. They expected it, no doubt. It belonged in the list of softening, sensuous influences peculiar to this home of Eastern luxury. It was softening enough, certainly, but its application was not happy. They now gave me a pair of wooden clogs—benches in miniature, with leather straps over them to confine my feet (which they would have done, only I do not wear No. 13s.). . . .

They put me in another part of the barn and laid me on a stuffy sort of pallet, which was not made of cloth of gold, or Persian shawls, but was merely the unpretending sort of thing I have seen in the negro quarters of Arkansas. There was nothing whatever in this dim marble prison but five more of these biers. It was a very solemn place. I expected that the spiced odours of Araby were going to steal over my senses now, but they did not. A copper-coloured skeleton, with a rag around him, brought me a glass decanter of water, with a lighted tobacco pipe in the top of it, and a pliant stem a yard long, with a brass mouth-piece to it.

Around Galata Tower, 1852
Théophile Gautier

In Paris the idea of going for a walk between eight and eleven at night in Pere-Lachaise or the cemetery at Montmartre would strike one as ultra-singular and cadaverously Romanticist; it would make the boldest dandies quail, and as for the ladies, the mere suggestion of such a party of pleasure would make them faint with terror. At Constantinople no one thinks twice about it. The fashionable walk of Pera is situated on the crest of the hill on which lies the Little Field. A frail railing, broken down in several places, forms between the Field of Death and the lively promenade a line of demarcation which is crossed constantly. A row of chairs and tables, at which are seated people drinking coffee, sherbet, or water, runs from one end to the other of the terrace, that forms an elbow farther on and joins the Great Field behind Upper Pera. . . .

At either end of the terrace there is a café concert, where one can enjoy with one's refreshments the pleasure of hearing an open-air orchestra of gipsies performing German waltzes, or overtures to Italian operas.

This tomb-bordered promenade is uncommonly gay. The incessant music—for one orchestra starts up when another stops—imparts a festive air to the daily meeting of idlers, whose soft chatter forms a sort of bass to the brass phrases of Verdi.

Midnight in Pera, 1876
Pierre Loti

My house in Pera was situated in a secluded spot over-looking the Golden Horn and the distant panorama of the Turkish city. The splendour of summer lent charm to my abode; seated by my large, open window, study-ing the language of Islam, I would let my gaze hover above old Stamboul lying bathed in sunlight. Away in the background, in a grove of cypress trees, Eyoub came into view; it would have been heaven to be hidden with her there in that mystical forgotten place where our life would have lit upon its own strangely delightful setting.

All around my house, were immense stretches of land with nothing but cypresses and tombs—empty terrain where I spent more than one night with my mind bent on careless adventures with Armenian or Greek girls. . . .

Midnight! the fifth hour, according to Turkish clocks; the nightwatchmen are striking the ground with their heavy, iron-shod staves. In the Galata quarter the dogs are in revolt and the howling down there is appalling. The dogs in this neighbourhood remain strictly neutral, and I'm obliged to them for that; they are asleep hodge-podge outside my door. All is peace and quiet. In the three hours I've spent stretched out by my open window I've been watching the lights go out one by one. . . .

Yet all is quiet in Constantinople . . . . At eleven o'clock some cavalry and artillery went past my house at the gallop, heading for Stamboul; then from the batteries came muffled rumbling which petered out in the distance, and then everything fell silent again.

Owls are hooting in among the cypresses; they sound exactly as they do at home. I love this sound of summertime; it takes me back to woods in Yorkshire, to the beautiful evenings I spent under the trees at Brightbury.

Here, surrounded by all this stillness, images from the past come alive again, images of all that is shattered and gone, never to return.

Theatre in Pera, 1843
Gérard de Nerval

Since I, unlike the Mussulmans, was under no obligation to sleep all day and spend the whole night in pleasure during the blessed month of Ramadan, that combination of Lent and Carnival, I often went to Pera to keep in touch with the Europeans. One day my eyes were startled by the sight of a theatre bill ported on the walls, announcing the opening of a theatrical season. An Italian company was about to open for three months, and the name which shone forth in large letters as that of the dramatic tar of the moment was that of the Ronzi-Tacchinardi, that prima donna of Rossini's best period to whom Stendhal devoted several fine pages. Alas, Ronzi was no longer young. She came to Constantinople as the famous tragedienne Mile. Georges had done, some years before, who, after appearing at the Pera theatre and also before the Sultan, had gone to play in the Crimea, to play Iphigenia in Tauris in that very place where once the temple of Thoas rose. Eminent artists, like great geniuses of every kind, have a profound feeling for the past. They enjoy the pleasures of adventure, and the Eastern sun seems to draw them to itself, as though they felt themselves to be endowed with the nature of eagles. Donizetti was to conduct the orchestra, by special permission of the Sultan, to whom he had been for some time master of the music.

The City as Hell

Not all its visitors loved Istanbul, but even those who hated it expressed their feelings in a way that seems to take inspiration from the city's rich and elaborate character.

Hating Constantinople, 1914
André Gide

Constantinople justifies all my prejudices and joins Venice in my personal hell. As soon as you admire some bit of architecture, the surface of a mosque, you learn (and you suspected it already) that it is Albanian or Persian. Everything was brought here, as to Venice, even more than to Venice, by sheer force or by money. Nothing sprang from the soil itself; nothing indigenous underlies the thick froth made by the friction and clash of so many races, histories, beliefs, and civilisations.

The Turkish costume is the ugliest you can imagine; and the race, to tell the truth, deserves it.

Oh Golden Horn, Bosporus, shore of Scutari, cypresses of Eyoub! I am unable to lend my heart to the most beautiful landscape in the world if I cannot love the people that inhabit it. . . .

The joy of leaving Constantinople, the praises of which I shall have to leave to others. Laughing sea in which the dolphins rejoice. Charm of the Asiatic shores; great trees near by under which the herds seek out shade.

The End of Istanbul, 1850
Gustave Flaubert

The East will soon be nothing but a question of sun. At Constantinople most of the men are dressed in the European fashion, operas are played, there are reading rooms, milliners' shops, etc. A hundred years hence the harem, gradually invaded by intercourse with Frankish ladies, will crumble to dust of itself under the leading article and the comic opera . . . . Soon the veil, already slighter and slighter, will pass from the faces of the women, and with it Moslemism will fly away altogether. The number of pilgrims to Mecca diminishes day by day; the ulemas fuddle themselves like vergers. Voltaire is talked of! Everything here is breaking up, as with us. He who lives longest will laugh most!

The Writers

EDMONDO DE AMICIS (1846–1908) was an Italian novel- ist and journalist, best known for his children's novel, *Heart*.

HANS CHRISTIAN ANDERSEN (1805–75) was a Danish author, most famous for his fairy tales, including "The Little Mermaid," "The Snow Queen," and "The Emper- or's New Clothes."

MONSIEUR D'ANDRESEL was the French ambassador to Constantinople during the early eighteenth century.

4 **GIACOMO CASANOVA** (1725–98) was an Italian author and adventurer famous for his affairs with multiple women and men at home and abroad.

58 **CLARA ERSKINE CLEMENT** (1834–1916) was an American traveler and author of numerous books. Her travel destinations included Palestine, Europe, and Turkey.

37 **MASTER THOMAS DALLAM** (1570–1614) was an English organ-builder who traveled from London to Istanbul and delivered an organ to Sultan Mehmed III in 1600.

41, 68 **ARTHUR CONAN DOYLE** (1859–1930) was a British novelist and physician, whose most famous literary creation, Sherlock Holmes, was a favorite of the Ottoman sultan Abdülhamid.

13, 23, 31, 34, 49, 52, 55, 63, 68, 76, 94, 95, 101, 107, 111, 115 **HARRISON GRISWOLD DWIGHT** (1875–1959) was an American writer and diplomat born in Istanbul. He studied at Robert College and later lived in Washington. From 1935 to 1947 Dwight worked as assistant director of the Frick Collection in New York.

GRACE MARY ELLISON (d. 1935) was a British journalist and suffragette. Her 1915 book An Englishwoman in a Turkish Harem featured Ellison's essays published in the Daily Telegraph during her stay in a Turkish harem.

GUSTAVE FLAUBERT (1821–80) was a French novelist whose most famous work, *Madame Bovary*, put him in the dock with accusations of immorality.

THEOPHILE GAUTIER (1811–72) was a French poet, critic, and journalist, and one of the leading figures of the Romanticist movement.

ANDRE GIDE (1869–1951) was a French essayist, critic, and novelist who was awarded the Nobel Prize in Literature in 1947.

ERNEST HEMINGWAY (1899–1961) was an American writer famous for his economical prose style and his portrayal of the feelings of his country's lost generation.

32, 39 **AARON HILL** (1685–1750) was an English writer and dramatist. He wrote seventeen plays and published his *A Full and Just Account of the Present State of the Ottoman Empire* in 1709.

14 **LADY EMELIA HORNBY** was the wife of Sir Edmund Hornby, a British financial commissioner in the Ottoman Empire from August 1855 to 1856. Lady Hornby's *Constantinople during the Crimean War* features the letters she sent to her relatives during the time she spent in Constantinople.

105, 119, 128, 133 **PIERRE LOTI** (1850–1923) was a Romanticist writer and French navy officer whose love for Turkish culture and frequent visits to Istanbul resulted in the Turkish government's naming an Istanbul hill the Hill of Pierre Loti.

9, 29, 85 **HERMAN MELVILLE** (1847–91) was one of the most important American novelists of the nineteenth century. He published *Moby-Dick* in 1851 and *Bartleby, the Scrivener* in 1853.

WILL SEYMOUR MONROE (1863–1939) was an educator born in Pennsylvania. He studied at Paris, Leipzig, and Jena universities. He published *Turkey and the Turks* in 1907.

LADY MARY WORTLEY MONTAGU (1689–1762) was an English aristocrat. Her husband, Edward Wortley Montagu, was the British ambassador to Istanbul between 1716 and 1718. Montagu published her memoirs in *Letters from Turkey*.

GEORGINA MAX MÜLLER (1834–1919) was a writer and traveler and the wife of the German-born British philologist Max Müller.

GERARD DE NERVAL (1808–55) was the pen name of the Romanticist French poet and writer Gérard Labrunie, one of the most influential French authors of the nineteenth century.

LADY HESTER STANHOPE (1776–1839) was a British traveler who took a journey to Constantinople and the Middle East after a disappointing love affair.

ARTHUR SYMONS (1875–1945) was a British poet and critic, famous for his decadent verse and his contributions to leading modernist magazines of his time, including The Yellow Book.

MARK TWAIN (1835–1910) was the pen name of Samuel Langhorne Clemens, whose *The Adventures of Tom Sawyer* and *Adventures of Huckleberry Finn* are considered to be among the greatest works of American literature.

Bibliography

Amicis, Edmondo de, *Constantinople*, Merrill and Baker, New York, 1896.

Andersen, Hans Christian, *What the Moon Saw and Other Tales*, George Routledge and Sons, London, 1866.

d'Andresel, Monsieur, 1726 letter quoted in *The Tulip*, Anna Pavord, Bloomsbury, London and New York, 1999.

Casanova, Giacomo, *The Memoirs of Giacomo Casanova di Seingalt*, Casanova Society, London, 1922.

Clement, Clara Erskine, *Constantinople: The City of the Sultans*, Estes and Lauriat, Boston, 1895.

Dallam, Master Thomas, *Early Voyages and Travels in the Levant*, Hakluyt Society, London, 1893.

Doyle, Arthur Conan, *Memories and Adventures*, Little, Brown and Company, Boston, 1924.

Dwight, Harrison Griswold, *Constantinople Old and New*, Longmans, London, 1915.

Ellison, Grace Mary, *An Englishwoman in a Turkish Harem*, Methuen, London, 1915.

Gautier, Théophile, *The Travels of Théophile Gautier*, Little Brown, Boston, 1912.

Gide, André, *The Journals of André Gide*, Alfred A. Knopf, New York, 1948.

Hemingway, Ernest, "Old Constan," Toronto Daily Star, October 28, 1922. Quoted in *The Apprenticeship of Ernest Hemingway: The Early Years*, Charles A. Fenton, Farrar, Straus & Young, New York, 1954.

Hill, Aaron, *A Full and Just Account of the Present State of the Ottoman Empire in All Its Branches: With the Government, and Policy, Religion, Customs, and Way of Living of the Turks in General. Faithfully Related from a Serious Observation Taken in Many Years Travels through Those Countries*, G. Parker, London, 1733.

Hornby, Emelia B.M, *Constantinople during the Crimean War*, Richard Bentley, London, 1863.

Loti, Pierre, *Aziyade*, translation by William Needham, Creative Commons license 3.0, 2011, https://creativecommons.org/licenses/by/3.0/legalcode

Melville, Herman, *Journals: The Writings of Herman Melville, Vol. 15*, Northwestern University Press, Evanston, 1989.

Monroe, Will Seymour, *Turkey and Turks*, L. C. Page & Company, Boston, 1907.

Montagu, Mary Wortley, *Letters and Works of Lady Mary Wortley Montagu*, edited by Lord Wharncliffe, Henry G. Bohn, London, 1861.

Müller, Georgina Max, *Letters from Constantinople*, Longmans, Green, and Co., London, New York, and Bombay, 1897.

Nerval, Gérard de, *The Women of Cairo: Scenes of Life in the Orient*, Harcourt, Brace and Company, New York, 1930.

Stanhope, Hester, *Travels of Lady Hester Stanhope*, H. Colburn, London, 1846.

Symons, Arthur, "Constantinople," *Harper's Monthly Magazine*, May 1903.

Twain, Mark, *The Innocents Abroad, or The New Pilgrims' Progress*, H.H. Bancroft and Company, San Francisco, 1869.

Tarver, John Charles, *Gustave Flaubert as Seen in His Works and Correspondence*, D. Appleton, New York, 1895.

Acknowledgments

The editor and publisher acknowledge with thanks the permission to use material in this book from the following: Northwestern University Press for excerpts from Herman Melville's *Journals*, copyright © 1989 by Northwestern University Press and The Newbury Library. Bloomsbury Publishing Plc for use of the excerpt from the letter by Monsieur d'Andresel quoted in *The Tulip* (© Anna Pavord, 1999).

Illustration Sources

The illustrations in this volume are from: Thomas Allom, *Constantinople and the Scenery of the Seven Churches of Asia Minor published in two volumes with text by Robert Walsh* (London: Fisher, Son & Co, 1839): 3, 7, 15, 54, 61, 65, 71, 83, 87, 89, 91, 109, 129; Anna Bowman Dodd, *In the Palace of the Sultans* (London: William Heinemann, 1904): 112, 122, 136 (courtesy of the Rare Books and Special Collections Library of the American University in Cairo); Antoine Ignace Melling, *Voyage pittoresque de Constantinople et des rives du Bosphore* (Paris, London, 1819): 1, 5, 19, 24, 30, 34, 38, 98, 102, 120; Ignatius Mouradgea d'Ohsson, *Tableau Général de l'Empire Othoman, tome premier* (Paris, 1787): 62 (courtesy of the Rare Books and Special Collections Library of the American University in Cairo); Ja.s Whittle and R.H. Laurie, No. 53 Fleet Street, London (1818): 117.